Sinkholes

Sandra Friend

Pineapple Press, Inc.
Sarasota, Florida

To my friend and cheerleader "Dr. Fred" Bortz, for encouraging my enthusiasm about natural science writing and for helping me take the leap from curious student to author.

Inquiries should be addressed to:

Pineapple Press, Inc.
P.O. Box 3889
Sarasota, Florida 34230
www.pineapplepress.com

Library of Congress Cataloging-in-Publication Data

Friend, Sandra.
     Sinkholes / Sandra Friend.— 1st ed.
          p.   cm.
     Includes bibliographical references (p.).
     ISBN 1-56164-258-4 (alk. paper)
  1. Sinkholes. 2. Sinkholes—Pictorial works. I. Title.

     GB609.2 .F75 2002
     551.44'7—dc21

                                     2001058010

First Edition
10 9 8 7 6 5 4 3 2 1

Design by Shé Sicks
Printed in China

Table of Contents

Understanding Sinkholes 4
    What Is a Sinkhole? 4
    A World Full of Holes 6
    Who Cares about Sinkholes? 8
    Sinkhole or Not? 10
    Rocks That Dissolve 12
    From Rock to Landscape 14
    One Grain at a Time 16
    When Caverns Collapse 18
    All Stressed Out 20
    Inside a Sinkhole 22

Living Landscapes 24
    The World Below 24
    Nature's Sculptures 26
    Mountains and Bridges 28
    Valleys 30
    The Big Gulp 32
    Vanishing Act 34
    Seaworthy Sinkholes 36
    When Sinkholes Fill Up 38

Water 40
    The Water Cycle 40
    The Water Table 42
    Nature's Drainpipe 44
    Aquifers 46
    Natural Wells 48
    Springs 50
    Fresh Water under the Sea 52

Habitats 54
    The Sinkhole Community 54
    A Precious Pond 56
    Living in a Spring 58
    Cavern Dwellers 60
    At the Oasis 62

Living with Sinkholes 64
    In Ancient Times 64
    Spotting a Sinkhole 66
    When the Earth Yawns 68
    Filling a Sinkhole 70
    Careful Construction 72
    Guarding Against Collapse 74

Sinkholes in Our Midst 76
    Nature's Bounty 76
    Buried Treasure 78
    One Big Toilet 80
    Water: A Precious Resource 82
    Save That Sinkhole! 84
    A Natural Wonder 86

Where to Visit a Sinkhole 88
Additional Resources 90
Glossary 91
Index 93
Acknowledgments 95

What Is a Sinkhole?

A sinkhole is a
- hole in the earth's surface
- natural drain into the water table
- source of fresh water
- haven for marine life
- cavern's entrance
- cool microclimate sheltering plants and animals
- sudden collapse that can swallow a highway or a building

A sinkhole is a special type of hole in the ground. You can't dig a hole and call it a sinkhole. Sinkholes simply happen—sometimes very quickly.

One moment the ground looks fine. Seconds later, the soil begins to crack. Eventually a pit opens up where the ground used to be.

Sinkholes come in many shapes and sizes. They can be broad and shallow or deep and narrow. They can be jagged cracks in the ground or smooth-walled cylinders that look suspiciously like concrete pipes.

When a sinkhole happens suddenly, it's a natural disaster. It destroys its surroundings. But when the sinkhole stops growing, it becomes a permanent part of the landscape, a new and interesting environment to

This massive subsidence sinkhole in Wekiwa Springs State Park in Orlando, Florida, opened up over the course of several days, causing several enormous longleaf pines to flip over and point their lengthy tap roots at the sky. (Sandra Friend)

Typical sinkhole in the Hartland subdivision, Lexington, Kentucky. (James R. Rebmann, Photographer)

explore. A sinkhole may open up an entrance to a cavern or uncover a new source of fresh water. It may fill with water to become a permanent lake or pond.

New sinkholes appear every day. But most of the earth's sinkholes have been around for hundreds, thousands, even millions of years. They provide a special home for unusual plant and animal communities—and a special link between the earth's surface and our groundwater resources.

A large sinkhole opens near a home in Sylacauga, Alabama. (Paul Moser, Geological Survey of Alabama)

A World Full of Holes

Hundreds of millions of sinkholes exist on our planet, and more appear every day. They form in the deepest, darkest forests in Germany, on the steaming plains of Zambia, in the thick jungles of Belize, and on the steep mountains of Puerto Rico. They appear in the wilds of Vietnam and Laos, in the African Congo, and in the high mountains of Yugoslavia. Sinkholes hide in the Nullabor Plain of Australia, the wind-swept Arabian Desert, and the islands of the Mediterranean Sea. They drop through fossilized coral reef terraces in Japan. They appear in cold, snowy places too: on the outskirts of Moscow and in the Alaskan tundra. Sinkholes are even found in the ocean floor.

The United States has millions of sinkholes. Almost 75% of the continental United States has the right geology for sinkholes of one type or another to appear. These sinkholes lurk everywhere. You'll find them in the deserts of southern California, along the Pecos River in New Mexico, in the prairies of the Midwest, and in the pine forests of Maine, creating problems for land developers but unique opportunities for new ecological communities to develop.

Sinkholes within sinkholes—hikers within the Riva Skocjan park in Slovenia walk on the floor of a giant sinkhole, which contains a collapsed-roof sinkhole, forming a natural bridge far above their heads.
(Dave Bunnell)

Sinkholes commonly occur along the north coast of Puerto Rico. (W. H. Monroe, U.S. Geological Survey)

Cavers prepare to enter a cave through a mountaintop sinkhole in the wind-swept and jagged karst mountains of Carlista in northern Spain.(Dave Bunnell)

Who Cares about Sinkholes?

Until a sinkhole swallows a building, we don't tend to think about this phenomenon. But there are some professions for which poking around sinkholes is all part of a day's work.

Hydrologists, scientists who study water flow, concern themselves with the impact of sinkholes on our water supply. Since sinkholes can both provide and take away water, the presence of sinkholes greatly affects the quality and quantity of water passing through a region.

Geologists in sinkhole-prone areas spend a lot of time investigating new sinkholes. When construction begins in a sinkhole-prone area, geologists are called upon to determine whether it's safe to build in a certain spot. Even after a road or a building is in place, geologists may be able to determine whether the ground might collapse. Often a collapse happens without warning, and then it's up to the geologists and structural engineers to work together to determine what to do about the sinkhole and whether the building or road can be saved.

Paleontologists find ancient sinkholes rich with the bones of creatures that fell into the open pit. As time passed, layers of sand and mud washed into these sinkholes, filling them back up to ground level. It's a delight when a paleontologist finds a

Geologists inspect a sink that opened in the bottom of a holding pond near Tallahassee. (Harley Means, Florida Geological Survey)

new mud-filled sinkhole to explore. Bones of mammals and reptiles from the Pleistocene and Miocene epochs have been found in the strata of sinkholes. Archeologists study sinkholes too, finding artifacts from ancient civilizations.

Biologists study sinkholes to learn about the diversity of life in the sinkhole environment. Cave dwellers such as skinks and bats often live in sinkholes that connect to caverns. Most dry sinkholes contain a moist bottom, providing a cool home for plants and animals that would otherwise struggle to survive in the surrounding woods.

Conservationists and naturalists care about sinkholes. Construction in a sinkhole-prone region affects the quality of the water resources in the area. The very act of constructing roads and buildings may lead to more sinkholes. On public lands, the way sinkholes are managed affects the diversity of species in the area and the availability of these natural resources for recreation.

Geologist Paul Moser checks the depth of a fresh sinkhole in Alabama. (Bob Baker, Geological Survey of Alabama)

Sinkhole or Not?

A sinkhole is a naturally occurring disturbance in the landscape. But sometimes it's hard to tell if human activity triggered a sinkhole. Many ground collapses are labeled sinkholes when they actually belong to a more general category: subsidence. Subsidence occurs when the underlying support of a piece of land disappears. Perhaps coal miners tunneled too close to the surface, creating a hollow under a suburban yard. No one notices until years later, when, for example, an above-ground pool is installed and the additional weight of the water causes the ground underneath to collapse into the mine.

Drilling for water can result in subsidence, as can the presence of oil wells. Removing too much fluid from the ground without replacing it causes structural weakness in the rocks deep below our feet. Without the upward push of fluid pressure to keep the rocks together, they crumble and subsidence occurs. In California, parts of Long Beach, San Jose, and Los Angeles have dropped more than ten feet due to the withdrawal of oil or water under the cities, causing serious problems to underground utilities and shifting the foundations of buildings. Several square miles along Galveston Bay, Texas, sank more than three feet in the early 1920s after oil was withdrawn from the area. Groundwater withdrawn for use in oil refineries has resulted in another thirty feet of subsidence since the 1920s.

An overabundance of water can create subsidence as well. Water-

Cracked ground in a roadbed might signal an eroded drainpipe or a burst water main. But in a region prone to sinkholes, even simple cracks in the road must be investigated quickly.

(Sandra Friend)

main breaks in urban neighborhoods are notorious for causing the collapse of buildings. The unstoppable rush of water digs into the ground at such a great volume, it erodes everything in its path, causing a collapse.

Earthquakes also cause subsidence. An earthquake in 1898 caused several railroad buildings in Rosel, Kansas, to "disappear overnight," leaving behind a pond seventy feet deep. In regions with permafrost—where deep layers of the tundra are permanently frozen—a lack of insulation between heated oil pipelines or buildings and the cold ground can trigger a type of subsidence called thermokarst subsidence. When ice melts out of the soil, the surface of the ground collapses.

So how can you tell if a ground collapse is a sinkhole? Sinkholes require a special set of conditions to happen. They are part of the natural process of erosion, and true sinkholes occur in special types of easily dissolved rock found in regions called karst.

A Virginia house collapses into a sinkhole induced by water well drilling. (David A. Hubbard Jr., VDMME/DMR)

Rocks That Dissolve

Disappearing lakes, bubbling springs, and beautiful caverns are all a part of the weird and wonderful world of karst. Karst is a type of landscape that behaves quite differently than other sorts of landscapes. It's full of holes, cracks, and crevices. It soaks up water like a sponge. Its rock is always dissolving. And it's the only place where true sinkholes are born.

Karst is the name for any type of terrain where the bedrock dissolves easily. The name comes from a region in Slovenia, a country along the Adriatic Sea that is well known for its sinkholes, caverns, and other unusual geologic formations. In Slovenian, *kar* means cave and *arst* means oak tree. Oak trees and other acidic plants help to accelerate the erosion of the karst.

Can you tell if the ground under your feet is karst? Karst occurs over roughly 15% of the earth's surface. It's easy to recognize karst when there's no soil covering it. Bare karst surfaces look bizarre, since the epikarst—the etched surface of the karst—is visible. It consists of a network of tiny cracks, channels, fissures, and holes that soak up water. There are pits, grooves, pockmarks, cracks, and crevices everywhere. Karst has different names for different surface shapes. Flat, bare karst is known as a pavement. Karren is karst with deep crevices and jagged, pointed structures.

The bedrock in most areas with karst is protected by both soil and plants, which help slow down erosion. This is true for the Great Valley of the eastern United States. It's a vast region of karst extending from Pennsylvania to Alabama along the

Potholes in karst.
(Dave Bunnell)

Appalachian Mountains. The valley contains thousands of known caverns, and it's prone to sinkholes. When it rains, much of the water soaks into the karst, but dense soils, such as clay, also force water to follow gravity to form a stream or a pond. Since the Great Valley has streams and rivers, a lot of groundwater stays on the surface.

If you see a sinkhole, you're standing on karst. If you see a limestone cavern, you're standing on karst. But sinkholes and caverns are only two of the many unusual landforms found in karst. Some of the world's strangest geologic features occur only where you find karst.

Coastal karst on Island of Mallorca in the Mediterranean. (David A. Hubbard Jr.)

Lapies, a jagged karst formation, in the French Pyrenees. (David A. Hubbard Jr.)

From Rock to Landscape

For karst to form, water must be able to soak into the bedrock. The bedrock must be porous and permeable or have plenty of joints and bedding planes that water can seep down through. Karst can form in any kind of rock that meets these conditions, from chalk and gypsum to dolostone, a sedimentary rock made up of calcium and magnesium. Limestone, however, is the most common rock in which karst forms.

A sedimentary rock made up of the mineral calcite, limestone contains the remains of many small prehistoric organisms such as brachiopods, corals, and mollusks. Some types of limestone, such as oolite, are hard and bumpy and have visible fossil remains. Others , such as chalk, crumble easily because they have more soft plant remains than crushed shells and bones.

Sponges are porous. Karst acts like a sponge because it contains thousands of holes, cracks, crevices, and

In Greece, the picturesque shores of the Ionian Islands owe their unique beauty to the action of waves on karst. The tiny island of Paxos, just south of Corfu, boasts more sea caves per mile of coastline than anywhere else on earth. (Susan Friend)

fissures. For limestone to be permeable, those cracks and crevices must interconnect. When water permeates the porous surface of limestone, it disappears quickly into the ground. Other rocks don't act like this. If you pour water onto a slab of slate, it won't seep into the rock. It will flow to the edge and spill over. But if you pour water onto limestone in karst, it will soak right in. If the limestone is topped by tougher bedrock, such as shale, water will spread across the surface of the harder rock until it reaches a crevice. Small crevices widen into big cracks. Over thousands of years, these small crevices grow into cavities, and cavities grow into caves. As the cycle continues—the karst repeatedly dries out and then soaks up more water—the erosion accelerates. With cracks above and caves below, the karst weakens and collapses, creating a sinkhole.

Flowing partially underground during the dry season, a seasonal river in a Himalayan karst vanishes into a sinkhole at Devi Falls near Pokhara, Nepal.
(Sandra Friend)

One Grain at a Time

Solution-subsidence sinkholes occur gradually as part of the corrosion process that creates the karst landscape.

Limestone, the most common bedrock in karst, is made up of calcium carbonate, $CaCO_3$. When rainwater, H_2O, seeps through layers of leaves, pine needles, and soil on its way into the ground, it picks up carbon dioxide, CO_2, from the decaying matter, forming a mild acid known as carbonic acid, H_2CO_3 —the same acid found in soda pop!

As this acidic water trickles into and interacts with the limestone, it dissolves the bedrock, forming various ions that are carried off in the flow of groundwater. The acidic water easily etches pathways through the karst as it flows down to the water table. If the land is relatively flat, the solution will flow along joints in the rock, expanding their size. Humidity accelerates the corrosion. The deepest sinkholes tend to form in tropical regions.

Solution-subsidence sinkholes happen in places where there is little or no soil protecting the epikarst. As the bedrock dissolves, the ground above it lowers slowly, grain by grain, creating a broad, shallow depression. These bowl-like sinkholes are also called dolines, after the Slovakian word *dolina,* which describes their shape.

Depending on the existing channels in the bedrock, corrosion can also etch solution pipes. As water seeps downward, it gradually creates narrow, steep-sided sinkholes that widen over time. Solution pipes often look man-made, like perfectly formed concrete pipes.

Solution pipe along the bank of the Suwannee River in Suwannee County, Florida. (Harley Means, Florida Geological Survey)

A rolling sinkhole plain with many dolines drains into one of America's greatest natural wonders, Mammoth Cave. (Deanna Davis, Kentucky Geological Survey)

Aerial view of numerous shallow sinkholes in an agricultural region of the Mitchell Plateau in Indiana. (Samuel S. Frushour, Indiana Geological Survey)

When Caverns Collapse

Collapse sinkholes develop over a long period of time, then appear in a sudden crash. They occur when the roof of a cavern or cavity collapses. A change in the water table is often the culprit. When heavy rains and flooding cause the water table to rise, the water level pushes hard against the tops of caverns, digging away at the soft bedrock. Water in a high water table moves quickly, and the increased velocity of water movement speeds up erosion.

Too little water is just as problematic. Water supports at least 40% of the weight of the roof of a water-filled cavern. As the water table drops, the support is no longer there to hold the cavern roof up—and it collapses, forming a sinkhole.

Collapse sinkholes happen most frequently when the water table falls or rises in a dramatically short period. A collapse sinkhole usually has a funnel shape, and its edges are jagged and irregular.

On the island of Kauai, Hawaii, the Queen's Bath is a littoral sinkhole in basalt, a collapse of a cavern's roof into a wave-cut sea cave. Littoral sinkholes are considered pseudokarst, or "fake" karst, since the bedrock itself did not dissolve to encourage the formation of the sinkhole.
(Dave Bunnell)

Inside a cavern, looking up, it doesn't feel like a sinkhole. From the forest floor, this gaping pit is evidence of a cavern roof collapse. This sinkhole formed in a region with a heavy concentration of caves within the Withlacoochee State Forest near Inverness, Florida. (Sandra Friend)

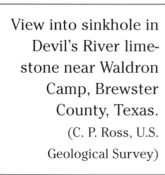

View into sinkhole in Devil's River limestone near Waldron Camp, Brewster County, Texas. (C. P. Ross, U.S. Geological Survey)

All Stressed Out

The most common type of sinkhole is the subsidence sinkhole. It forms during a geologic process called ravelling, when clay, silt, and sand filter into the ground through cracks in the karst. Rain accelerates the process by pushing large amounts of soil into the ground. As the cracks fill with these heavier, compacted materials, the weak bedrock collapses underground. A bowl-shaped depression appears in the ground above. As more dirt and sand wash into the bowl, it finally collapses under its own weight, creating a deep cone-shaped sinkhole. A subsidence sink-hole tends to be about twice as wide as it is deep.

The weight of water, buildings, roads, and heavy construction equipment can also force the appearance of a subsidence sinkhole. All it takes is the additional weight on the surface to cause a sinkhole that has been slowly forming to suddenly collapse. The collapse itself, however, is never quite the end of the sinkhole. Ravelling continues. Material keeps creeping downward through the karst until it fills up—or collapses again.

The employees at a Porsche dealership in Winter Park, Florida, noticed a little sinkhole in their parking lot one night. By the next morning, the sinkhole had swallowed a whole city block! Part of the car dealership, its cars, a truck, a house, and even a swimming pool slid down into the gaping hole.
(Florida Geological Survey Archives)

Aerial view of newly formed sinkhole near Orlando, probably taken during the mid-1960s. Notice the fence in the upper right corner for a comparison of size. (Florida Geological Survey Collection, Florida State Archives)

The "December Giant" collapse in Shelby County, Alabama, also known as the "Golly Hole," occurred on December 2, 1972. It's thought to be one of the largest sinkholes in the United States. At 350 feet wide, 450 feet long, and 150 feet deep, it's big enough to gobble up twelve football fields! (U.S. Geological Survey)

Inside a Sinkhole

No matter how slowly or quickly a sinkhole forms, it contains certain features common to every type of sinkhole. Although sinkholes can take on a wide variety of sizes and shapes, the typical sinkhole cuts a circular or oval hole in the earth, narrowing as it deepens. Collapse and solution-subsidence sinkholes can be rough around the edges, but they too tend to get narrow at depth. Sinkholes also change shape with age. The steep sides of a fresh collapse sinkhole eventually erode, making the hole broader.

A sinkhole acts as a funnel. Gravity draws water and soil down over its rim, and debris then slides down into the sinkhole's constricted throat. If the throat clogs up, the sinkhole will fill with material. When the clog disappears, the sinkhole continues to swallow debris into a natural piping system leading directly into cavities in the bedrock. Water, soil, and sand continue to flow downward until all cavities are filled and the erosion around the edges of the sinkhole stabilizes.

A sinkhole often grows broader as it grows older. If the sinkhole throat clogs, a pond or lake can form.
(Sandra Friend)

Nearly a hundred feet below the surface of the forest, the bottom of the Wekiwa Springs sinkhole intersects the water table. A pool of water formed in the sinkhole, even though there had been no rain in weeks. (Sandra Friend)

Sinkhole with outcropping of limestone bedrock. (Samuel S. Frushour, Indiana Geological Survey)

The World Below

Sinkholes lead to amazing wonders beneath the earth's surface. Imagine the surprise of the first explorers to New Mexico's Lechuguilla Cave when they attempted to discover why strong winds blew out of a sinkhole near Carlsbad Caverns! They found a cave even bigger than Carlsbad, with more unusual and complex formations. More than one hundred miles of passages have been mapped in Lechuguilla to date.

Through sinkholes, vast quantities of water enter the karst, broadening and deepening existing cavities to create caves. This slow dissolving of the bedrock also occurs near the water table, the level at which groundwater fully saturates the rock. As the water table drops or air seeps into the cave through a crevice or a sinkhole, the rock stops dissolving since the fizzy carbon dioxide that fuels the process can now escape.

What's hiding under those sinkholes in Florida? At Florida Caverns State Park, virtually all of the sinkholes have been explored, including those that lead to these incredibly beautiful caverns. (Sandra Friend)

At Pennsylvania's Lincoln Caverns, this sinkhole led to the discovery of the Whisper Rocks Cave. With a people-friendly entrance created for the cavern tour, the sinkhole now serves as an easy entrance and exit point for the bats that live in the cave. (Sandra Friend)

At the time Luray Caverns was discovered, the U.S. was caught in "cave frenzy." Entrepreneurs dug into the bottoms of sinkholes, looking for the next big tourist attraction that could top the splendors of Kentucky's Mammoth Cave. Luray was the result of such a business effort. Three local men found the caverns in 1878; within a few months they had opened it to the public. Journalists' reports of the colossal cavern brought tourists by the trainload. (Sandra Friend)

Nature's Sculptures

Deep within the earth, the processes of dissolution and deposition work hand-in-hand to create amazing natural sculptures. How do sinkholes fit in? They channel air and water into the karst. As water seeps into a sinkhole, dissolving the sinkhole's walls and fractures in the rock, it picks up minerals and creates an acidic solution. When carbon dioxide escapes from this solution underground, calcite crystals remain. Calcite is the crystalline form of limestone. Calcite crystals left behind from water dripping through the bedrock form magnificent formations in stone.

Shenandoah Caverns in Virginia boast some of the world's largest examples of "cave bacon," a type of ribbon flowstone formation in which the darker stripes are colored by iron within the calcite. (Sandra Friend)

Stalactites can be as thin as soda straws or as thick as a drum. Colored by iron, these squat stalactites in Florida Caverns look like the undersides of turnips growing through the cavern ceiling. (Sandra Friend)

Glistening white from the purity of the calcite, these formations in Seneca Caverns in West Virginia include stubby stalagmites, waterfall-like white flowstone, and tiny rimstone dams. (Sandra Friend)

Beautiful crystals can form from the deposition of calcium carbonate in a dry environment. Thick mud blocked the entrance to the chamber that these crystals grew in, forming a vacuum seal. When explorers opened the chamber, they marveled at the thousands of delicate aragonite flowers. The cave was opened to the public as Skyline Caverns in Virginia. (Sandra Friend)

Mountains and Bridges

Many Chinese paintings show pointed mountains that rise up out of a flat plain or inland sea. These small mountains are tower karst—tall, jagged hills with steep slopes. These rocky peaks are the remains of the land that once stood between ancient sinkholes in a higher plateau. Erosion cut the sinkholes apart, leaving towers of stone. The tallest tower karst hills in Kwangsi Province are 650 feet tall.

China's tower karst scenery attracts tourists from all over the world. For nearly 50 miles, tower karst rises along the banks of the Li River between Guilin and Yangsuo. In Yunnan, a mysterious tropical rock forest resulted from karst dissolution. The crevices between the tall rock pinnacles are no more than 90 feet wide.

A haystack hill is a blobby, rounded mountain, a form of cockpit karst. Haystack hills appear in humid tropical regions such as Puerto Rico, Jamaica, and New Guinea. They look like green gumdrops set flat side down and crowded tightly together on a plate. Cockpit karst also formed through slow erosion of the surrounding sinkholes in a level plain. In Puerto Rico, the hills, called *pepinos* or *mogotes*, rise 200 to 300 feet high. In Cuba, haystack hills reach as high as 1,000 feet. Haystack hills are often

Natural Bridge in Virginia is a gigantic natural bridge formation, the remains of an ancient sculpted karst.
(Sandra Friend)

Haystack hills in Poland.
(David A. Hubbard Jr.)

peppered with caverns. Sometimes a cave forms at the base of a haystack hill or tower karst. These caves can swallow passing streams and spit them out the other side of the mountain.

The arching form of a natural bridge calls to mind its formation from sinkholes and caverns. Most natural bridges we see have dissolved so greatly that little remains of the original sinkhole or cave.

Tower karsts along the Li River, Guilian, China.
(Maria Brooks)

Valleys

Sinkholes have an unusual effect on the shaping of valleys. In karst, sinkholes serve as a natural plumbing system. Water doesn't run aboveground—it drops into sinkholes and flows through caverns, popping up again as springs.

An aquitard is any obstruction that stops water flow. Since water can disappear and reappear from karst, a dead-end cliff is no obstruction for a stream. In karst, the water goes underground to get around it. A blind valley exists where the valley ends abruptly at a towering cliff wall, but the streams continue. Sometimes you'll hear a blind valley called a sinking valley, because the stream sinks down to the lowest point in the valley and disappears. The water emerges on the other side of the obstruction into a pocket valley, also called a steephead. In North Yorkshire, Great Britain, the River Aire pops up at the bottom of a 328-foot-tall limestone cliff that forms the upper end of a pocket valley. When water rises from karst on its own, it's called a resurgence.

A dry valley has no streams aboveground. All water drains into the karst. When the water table drops below a dry valley, new sinkholes form at the lowest point in the valley. When adjoining sinkholes merge, the resulting depression is called an *uvala.*

These rolling karst hills and valleys in Yugoslavia contain thousands of sinkholes. (David A. Hubbard Jr.)

Rolling karst plain near Park City, Kentucky. When drainage from the sinkhole temporarily blocked up, the sinkhole pond formed.

(Jim Currens, Lexington, KY)

Ancient sinkholes in the Appalachian and Allegheny Mountains created deep, mountain-cutting uvalas in West Virginia and Maryland.

One type of karst valley is called a *polje*. Poljes are common along the Adriatic Sea and in humid tropical regions. Their name comes from the Slavic word for field. Hills or mountains surround poljes, and there is no way for water to enter or exit the valley except as rain or through the karst. Although a polje may have a surface stream, the water eventually drains into the ground through a swallow hole called a *ponor*, the Slavic term for sink.

A solution pan is a shallow, flat basin in karst. Water seeps through the bottom of the pan. Swamps and small ponds form in solution pans, dependent on rainfall to keep from drying out. Deep, narrow gorges can also form in karst. Vikos, the "Grand Canyon of Greece," is more than 1,000 feet deep and 1,500 feet across, cutting through a barren karst.

Sinks of the Gandy Cave in Randolph County, West Virginia, a classic example of a sinking stream and a swallow hole cave entrance.

(Jim Currens, Lexington, KY)

The Big Gulp

We know that sinkholes can open up suddenly and swallow a park, a lake, or a house. But there is special type of sinkhole called a swallow hole that swallows water on a regular basis. A swallow hole may also be called a swallet, a riversink, or a ponor. These sinkholes drain whole bodies of flowing water into the karst. One of the world's largest swallow holes is the Gaping Ghyll in Yorkshire, Great Britain. A stream, Fell Beck, falls 350 feet down a shaft into the hole—the height of a 26-story building! At Cass Cave in West Virginia, a swallow hole gulps a stream into a pit 140 feet deep.

In karst, it's not unusual for a valley to end abruptly at a seemingly impassible obstruction. But water can always find a way through. It may soak into the karst, becoming a losing, or sinking, stream. There are many losing streams above the thousand caverns of the Ozarks in southern Missouri. A losing stream gradually soaks into the karst as it flows along until the stream simply vanishes for lack of water.

In a karst where soft rock and harder rock meet, water will attempt to dive down into the softer rock rather than excavate a new channel through the tougher rock—and off it goes, into the swallow hole.

A dry channel funnels storm water to this swallow hole when it rains. (Samuel S. Frushour, Indiana Geological Survey)

The Chipola River, north of Marianna, Florida, drops into a 90-foot-deep riversink, vanishing underground for a quarter of a mile within Florida Caverns State Park.

(Sandra Friend)

DISAPPEARING RIVER

HERE THE CHIPOLA RIVER FLOWS UNDERGROUND THROUGH A CAVERN AND REAPPEARS 1/4 MILE TO YOUR LEFT. THIS MAY BE COMPARED TO A SPRING WATER ENTERS THE GROUND AT A HIGH ELEVATION AND REAPPEARS AT A LOWER ELEVATION. DURING HICH WATER PART OF THE RIVER CONTINUES TO FLOW ABOVE THE GROUND IN A MAN MADE DITCH ONCE USED TO FLOAT LOGS DOWN STREAM. CHIPOLA MEANS SWEET IN THE CHOCTAW LANGUAGE.

The St. Marks River vanishes into a swallow hole south of Tallahassee, Florida. Before bridges were built across the St. Marks, the resulting natural bridge created a corridor for travel. During the Civil War, the Battle of Natural Bridge, fought at this spot in March 1865, kept Florida's capital from falling into Union hands.

(Sandra Friend)

Vanishing Act

Piled high with oranges and grapefruit, the steamboat *Chacala* chugged slowly across Alachua Lake towards its destination in Gainesville, Florida. It was 1891, and steamboats were still a novelty. Kids waved from the shore as they watched the boat shrink into the distance. Suddenly, the steamboat ran aground. The captain dashed out onto the deck to survey the problem. The steamboat was stuck in the mud. As the crew watched, the lake waters receded towards Gainesville, then vanished. Thousands of fish flopped around in the muck, gasping for water. The captain and his crew had to leave their ship behind and slog their way to shore.

Folks knew that the water in the lake rose and fell because of a sink-hole at the bottom of the lake, but this time it seemed like someone had pulled the drain plug out! Sure enough, when people explored the Alachua Sink, they discovered that the sinkhole's big plug of wood, dirt, and rocks was gone. The lake had drained in less than two hours. The area became a swampy prairie, dependent on rainfall for survival.

A sinkhole that takes water out of a lake is called a sink, although it acts more like a drain. Lakes with sinks in them may disappear, then reappear, thanks to the spongelike nature of karst. It can both soak up water and squeeze it out. And although fresh-

In 1865, George Thompson, an inspector for the Freedman's Bureau, visited Alachua Sink near Gainesville as the sink swallowed water from Paynes Prairie. Thompson wrote, "The entire surface of the water was completely covered with dead fish and alligators. So numerous were they that the sound of their gasping resembled the noise of a heavy shower of rain." (Collection of the P. K. Yonge Library of Florida History, University of Florida)

Lake Jackson, near Tallahassee, Florida, has a long history of disappearing and reappearing. The lake vanishes every 25 years or so, only to return after a few years. This 1932 photo shows the sinkhole surrounded by a sea of mud. (Herman Gunter, Florida Geological Survey Collection, Florida State Archives)

water springs emerge from sinkholes in karst, these same springs can act as drains when the water table is low. The water pressure within the earth can force a swallow hole to become a spring and vice versa. These reversible sinks, which geologists call by the French geologic term *estavelle*, change their direction of flow (swallow or discharge) based on fluctuations in the water table.

A more recent view of Porter Sink in Lake Jackson, taken in the fall of 2000. (Harley Means, Florida Geological Survey)

Seaworthy Sinkholes

Sinkholes have been forming on the earth's surface throughout all of geologic time. Ancient sinkholes predate humankind, and many of them have refilled with debris. They hide beneath our feet, packed full of rocks, soil, and sand.

Many of these ancient sinkholes sit at the bottom of the world's oceans. These ocean floor sinkholes are called blue holes, named for the dark blue spots the deep sinkholes make in otherwise shallow water. Hundreds of blue holes sit off the Atlantic coast of Florida. They formed during the Oligocene, Eocene, and early Miocene eras, when land that is now underwater was still above sea level. Many of them have partially refilled with sediment, such as one huge sinkhole off the coast of Key Largo, Florida, which is more than 2,000 feet in diameter.

Blue holes lie below Australia's Great Barrier Reef and are found in the depths of the Pacific Ocean around Okinawa, Japan, and the Bikini and Truk Islands. They lurk in the Gulf of Mexico off the coasts of Belize and Mexico and appear in the deep Adriatic Sea. The world's largest blue hole—at least 1,000 feet across and 460 feet deep—is suspected to be

Blue hole, San Salvador Island, Bahamas. (David A. Hubbard Jr.)

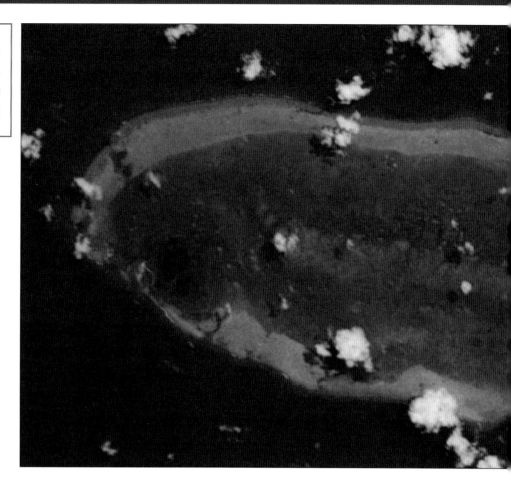

Lighthouse Reef, Belize. The Blue Hole (lower left), as seen from the space shuttle. (NASA)

one off the coast of Belize. Although blue holes are usually found under-water, some of the islands of the Bahamas contain deep blue holes. In these holes, a layer of fresh water lies on top of intruding salt water.

When Sinkholes Fill Up

When a dry sinkhole sits empty for a while, it begins to fill up with natural debris—loose sand, dirt, and rocks. Eventually, the sinkhole may disappear from view. But the sinkhole is still a sinkhole—still an unusual depression in the earth, still prone to collapse and dissolution in a karst environment.

What happens when a heavy object rests on one of these sinkholes? If the sinkhole was filled with soft sand or loose soil, it may act like a giant trap. Tractors and heavy farm equipment have fallen into these hidden sinkholes. Because of their weight, construction vehicles are at risk of disappearing into sinkholes during highway building through karst terrain.

Other sinkholes are filled with sturdier stuff. Miners quickly turned their attention to sinkholes in the Missouri Valley when they discovered the sinkholes were full of iron ore minerals. Thick mud might preserve fossils in a sinkhole. Sinkholes that have been filled with loose gravel thanks to glacial movement can be mined for gravel. Digging into a buried sinkhole and taking core samples can help geologists better understand the passage of geologic time.

Many sinkholes simply fill up with water. Seen from the air, it's apparent that most lakes in central Florida are water-filled sinkholes.

A Florida Geological Survey drill rig was unexpectedly swallowed by a sinkhole. (Florida Geological Survey Archives)

View from the space shuttle of central Florida's sinkhole lakes. (NASA)

The Water Cycle

Water constantly moves above, on, and below the surface of the earth. The overall amount of water always stays the same—it just changes its role as it travels through the hydrologic, or water, cycle.

Water evaporates from oceans, lakes, and rivers, rising into the sky to form clouds, giant masses of water droplets. Pushed by the wind, clouds move vast distances. Eventually, rain falls from the clouds, soaking back into the land and rejoining the oceans, lakes, and rivers. Water seeps down through the earth's soils and bedrock to form great reservoirs underground; trees transpire water into the air, creating haze across sunny forests. Icebergs, icecaps, and glaciers lock up millions of tons of water, which they return to the system as they melt and remove from the cycle as they re-form. Water rises, water falls, trickling down cliffs into streams that reach the oceans, a never-ending cycle.

Why are sinkholes important to the water cycle? At least 25% of the world's population gets its water from karst, and in karst, sinkholes provide the largest avenues down to the water table. Water shapes karst, and, in turn, karst affects the storage

Karst waters seep to the surface through spring vents in the upper Apalachicola River in Florida, just below the Woodruff Dam. These small vents are visible only when the river is low. (Harley Means, Florida Geological Survey)

Rainfall on karst seeps into the earth to continue its journey through the water cycle. But spongy karst can't always hold all of the water sent its way, especially after a heavy rain. These Indiana homes are at great risk of flooding because of their location—improperly placed within a low, broad sinkhole. The dike behind the homes traps some of the runoff from heavy rains. A pump removes the water that spills over the dike.
(Samuel S. Frushour, Indiana Geological Survey)

and purity of groundwater. No other landscape is tied so closely to the water cycle as karst. The simple act of water moving across karst causes the rock to dissolve, enlarging openings and passageways in the rock and releasing chemicals that neutralize the acidity of the water. Water flows at many different rates through karst, pooling in reservoirs or scouring and creating channels through the stone as it seeks out the water table. Entire streams and rivers flow underground in karst. Because water moves quickly through karst, problems with water quality spread quickly and often cover vast regions.

The Water Table

As water trickles down through soil, sand, and rock, it attempts to cling to other drops of water. Eventually, the water reaches a level where it is able to pool together, fully saturating the rock. The top of this saturated level is called the water table.

In other terrain, water circulates around grains of sand or soil in the saturation zone. But in karst, it fills the joints, crevices, and cracks of the rock. So the rise and fall of the water table plays an important role in karst—it creates sinkholes.

Too much water—in the form of excessive rainfall and sudden flooding, for example— can add extreme amounts of water to the water table, causing underground erosion to accelerate and triggering sinkholes. Conversely, when the water table drops, it can no longer support the weight of cavern roofs. Weak roofs can then collapse. When fallen roofs occur near the earth's surface, they cause sinkholes. A lack of rainfall for a long period of time will cause the water table to drop, as will the excessive removal of water from an area. Too much new construction—with a well tapping water for every new home—can lead to sinkholes. Subsidence sinkholes caused by water usage tend to be small but numerous. In one instance in Tampa, Florida, 64 sinkholes opened up within a two-mile radius of a new well.

Mining affects the water table and can lead to sinkhole formation. When mines are dug, they quickly fill back up with water. Pumps remove the water to make it safe for the miners

If water is improperly routed into karst, it will accelerate the growth of sinkholes. This retention pond near Gainesville, Florida, shows a sinkhole under development.
(Sandra Friend)

Many sinkholes intersect the water table. This one in the Leon Sinks Natural Area near Tallahassee, Florida, forms a permanent steep-walled pond.
(Sandra Friend)

to work. This procedure, called dewatering, often triggers multiple sinkholes. It removes so much water at the water table so quickly that karst weakens in many places, making it prone to sudden collapse. In 1962, dewatering caused a tragic disaster at a South African gold mine when a factory building collapsed into a subsidence sinkhole, killing 36 people.

Dewatering caused this large sinkhole to open up over a gypsum mine in Virginia. (James A. Lovett, VDMME/DMR)

Nature's Drainpipe

Since karst easily soaks up water, karst regions have few aboveground streams or rivers. Instead, water tends to seep underground, flowing towards the water table. As the largest surface features of karst, sinkholes act as drainpipes, swallowing whatever water flows into their depths.

Sinkholes often tip the balance between aboveground water sources (lakes, rivers, and ponds) and water below the ground. When the water table is high, water may push up out of a sinkhole to form a pond or lake. When the water table is low, the sinkhole may drain the water source. If the sinkhole clogs up with debris, it may artificially retain water until the debris washes away or the sinkhole grows larger.

When people rely on sinkholes to drain the landscape, clogged sinkholes can be a tragedy. Terrible floods have occurred when enough debris has washed into a sinkhole to plug the natural drain. In 1979, Jamaica experienced deadly flooding when a sinkhole in the Cave River Basin became blocked by loose soil eroding from an agricultural region.

Yet unplugged sinkholes are adept at swallowing large amounts of water. In the fall of 2000, a sinkhole in the bottom of Orange Lake, near Gainesville, Florida, slowly siphoned the lake in response to a dropping water table. Once covering 12,000 acres, the lake was reduced to 5,000 acres within a few months.

A sinkhole excavated and refilled to allow construction in the area shows resurgence (water rising to the surface from within the karst) after a little rain. (James R. Rebmann, Photographer)

Springs can turn deadly when water rises quickly within karst. Donaldson Cave at Spring Mill State Park in Indiana during flood stage. (Samuel S. Frushour, Indiana Geological Survey)

This country road in Logan County, Kentucky, frequently floods due to a nearby sinkhole. (Jim Currens, Lexington, KY)

Water often settles in the low areas created by sinkholes, causing flooding, as in this Virginia backyard. (David A. Hubbard Jr., VDMME/DMR)

Aquifers

Aquifers are underground reservoirs that provide a reliable source of water. Aquifers occur where water becomes trapped beneath layers of impermeable rock. The surface of the water in the aquifer is the top of the water table. The water may be trapped in beds of gravel or permeable rock beneath a cap of less permeable bedrock. Aquifers in karst, however, trap water in the holes, grooves, and channels in the bedrock itself and in networks of interconnected caverns. They tend to be tightly connected to the water cycle. Prolonged drought makes the water levels fall; flooding increases the capacity of the aquifer.

The Floridan and Biscayne Aquifers provide drinking water for most of Florida. In Texas, the Edwards Aquifer furnishes drinking water to people from Austin to San Antonio. The Roswell Aquifer in New Mexico supplies fresh water to towns in the arid desert. The Yucatan Peninsula of Mexico has an immense aquifer that extends under the Gulf of Mexico in places. This aquifer is the only source of fresh water for the Yucatan; there are no streams, lakes, or rivers hiding in the Yucatan's jungles. Water-filled sinkholes in the Yucatan, called *cenotes,* provide access to the Yucatan Aquifer. The world's deepest *cenote* is thought to be Zacatón, near Tampico, Mexico, at 1,080 feet deep.

The Floridan Aquifer is perhaps the most well known karst aquifer on earth. The aquifer is enormous, underlying almost 100,000 square miles of the southeastern United States. It replenishes, or recharges, with water when rain falls on karst where the aquifer lies near the surface, particularly in north central Florida, southern Alabama, and southern Georgia. Scientists come from afar to study the mysteries of the Floridan Aquifer, particularly in the recharge region south of Tallahassee known as the Woodville Karst Plain. Since the 1950s, cave divers have been exploring the aquifer under the Woodville Karst, using the many sinkholes and springs in the area as entry points into its network of water-filled caverns.

Florida's second largest spring, Wakulla Springs, is one of the world's largest, discharging up to one billion gallons of water each day. Through its cavernous mouth 300 feet below the surface, teams of cave divers map the Floridan Aquifer in the Woodville Karst Plain. It's not an easy task. Special equipment has been developed to surmount the obstacles of staying underwater under the ground for such long distances, including re-breathers (which allow divers to reuse their exhaled air), long-range underwater scooters, special lighting, underwater radios, and sonar mapping devices. Thus far, the Woodville Karst Plain Project, which has overseen the project since the early 1990s, reports more than three miles of exploration along the main tunnel, the birthplace of Wakulla Springs.

(Sandra Friend)

Natural Wells

When a sinkhole intersects the water table, it allows easy access to clean, fresh water. Artesian wells happen when water pressure pushes water through a conduit to the surface. Besides a sinkhole, a conduit may be a cavern mouth, an intentionally drilled hole, a solution pipe, or a collection of small grooves and holes in the karst. Artesian wells tend to provide a constant pool of water at the surface.

Artesian wells are named for the region of Artois, France, where Carthusian monks first recorded their existence in the twelfth century. These natural wells provided fresh, warm water in a karst region. The only natural water sources in the Sahara and Arabian Deserts are artesian wells. These form oases, which attract lush plant life in the otherwise barren desert. Desert explorers report seeing dry sinkholes in the sand surrounding oases, perhaps the remains of dried-up wells. During the reign of King Solomon, Jerusalem's water source was the "springs of Harub in the Hebron Hills," a group of karst springs. Modern-day Beirut draws water from the subterranean river of Jeita Cave.

Artesian pressure pushes water through the oddest of places, like this volcano-shaped structure inside Smoke Hole Caverns in West Virginia. Minerals suspended in the water cemented into place over time, creating the travertine cone that funnels the water's flow.
(Sandra Friend)

This spring in Virginia pushes groundwater to the surface with enormous artesian force.
(David A. Hubbard Jr.)

Florida has many sinkholes that fill with water to the brim, such as this one at Florida Caverns State Park near Marianna.
(Sandra Friend)

Springs

Springs provide an exit point for water to leave the aquifer and return to the surface. They typically form where there is a change in the permeability of the bedrock. Karst springs can vary from tiny seeps out of a wall of limestone and miniscule bubblers along the floor of a stream to enormous gushes of water rising from a cavern or sinkhole. Springs are classified in order of magnitude, depending on the volume of water they push out. The largest type of spring is a first-magnitude spring, where the water flow meets or exceeds a volume of 100 cubic feet per second.

Thanks to its karst terrain, Florida is one of the few places in the world with a large number of first-magnitude springs—27 in all, pouring out a combined flow of more than six billion gallons of water a day! Because of their funnel-like shape and proportional depth, it is easy to discern that many of Florida's springs pour

Water pours out of a blue spring in northern Spain. (Dave Bunnell)

This spring discharges water from a 20-square-mile region of Indiana's Mitchell Plateau. (Samuel S. Frushour, Indiana Geological Survey)

out of sinkholes, which may have been dry pits at an earlier point in geologic time. Florida has more than 300 major springs, with thousands of smaller springs adding to the water flow. Unlike artesian wells, which provide a pool of water at the surface, artesian springs bubble over and gush water out, which flows away to become a stream or river. Many of Florida's rivers start as artesian springs.

Springs are one of the most important features in karst. In ancient times, villages sprung up around karst springs, since they provided the only source of clear, fresh water in an area. Even today, springs continue to be a gathering place, not just for their water but also for the fish they attract and for recreation.

Fresh Water under the Sea

T here is at Aradus amid the sea,
Which bubbles out sweet water
and disparts
From round itself the salt waves;
and, behold,
In many another region the
broad main
Yields to the thirsty mariners
timely help,
Belching sweet waters forth
amid salt waves.

Although it may seem odd, artesian springs can be found in the ocean floor. As far back as 50 B.C., the Roman historian Titus Lucretius Carus wrote of this freshwater spring in the sea. Along Italy's western coastline, many submarine springs flood fresh water into the Adriatic Sea. Sailors in the Gulf of Mexico claimed they could drop a bucket into the sea off Cedar Key and scoop up drinking water. In fact, five different freshwater springs cluster near Cedar Key, providing a bounty for fishermen. Fish are attracted to the constant temperatures of freshwater springs under the sea.

These underwater artesian springs occur where aquifers extend out under the ocean, separated from seawater by water-resistant layers of rock. Fresh water emerges from deep sinkholes and crevices in the ocean floor, creating a unique and unusual environment for marine life. But just like certain sinkholes on land, they can suddenly change function, sucking seawater into the aquifer rather than pouring forth fresh water. The blue holes of the Bahamas are considered particularly treacherous because of strong eddy currents that can generate whirlpools strong enough to suck a boat to the ocean floor.

Freshwater submarine springs occur all over the world—from New York to California, from Bahrain to Barbados. Water pushing to the surface of the sea shows the boil of the spring and can be spotted easily when the tides are low.

Cave divers explore the depths of a freshwater spring. (Doug Stamm)

Florida's coastline boasts a number of submarine springs. Red Snapper Sink, 12 miles off the coast of Crescent Beach, is a favorite of deep-sea fishermen. Red snappers flock to this giant sinkhole, a funnel-shaped depression with a bottom nearly 464 feet below sea level. Another spring, Crescent Beach Submarine Spring, sits just off of Anastasia Island. A solitary spring, Mud Hole Submarine Spring, lies off of Sanibel Island. The state's other submarine springs are clustered around Cedar Key and Apalachicola Bay, with a lone spring near the mouth of the Choctawhatchee River.

The Sinkhole Community

The appearance of a sinkhole creates the foundation for a new ecosystem different from the surrounding forest, plain, or desert. A sinkhole provides a cool, damp environment, allowing atypical species to establish themselves. Any species of plant that can dig its tendril-like roots firmly into the slender joints and cracks found in limestone can grow easily in a sinkhole. The calcium-rich walls of a sinkhole attract plants that need an alkaline environment to survive, and the perpetual moisture of an old, stable sinkhole lures plants that love dampness and humidity, including mosses and many rare species of ferns. One of the rarest ferns in North America, the American Hart's-Tongue Fern, is found only in and around sinkholes, primarily in Tennessee.

Animals, too, find sinkholes to their liking. Small caverns opened up by collapse sinkholes can provide dens for mammals such as foxes, otters, wolves, and bears. Animals known as troglophiles can spend their entire lives in the cool, damp bottom of a sinkhole. These include certain species of crayfish, worms, spiders, beetles, and salamanders.

Gentle solution sinkholes puncturing the flatness of Florida's scrubby flatwoods give themselves away by the profusion of moisture-loving plants, particularly palmettos and ferns, attracted to the depressions. (Sandra Friend)

At Devil's Millhopper State Geologic Site, an enormous collapse sinkhole supports a set of vibrant ecosystems. Almost a dozen waterfalls of various heights and flows drop into this 120-foot-deep, 500-foot-wide sinkhole filled with lush vegetation. Walking into the pit is like stepping into the Amazon, with giant ferns and cool, moist mist filling the air along with the soothing sound of multiple cascades. Surrounding the sink is a deciduous Appalachian-style forest in the middle of Gainesville, Florida! Ferns, ivy, and mosses thrive in the Devil's Millhopper. (Sandra Friend)

This fox may find a suitable den within a collapse sinkhole. (Sandra Friend)

A Precious Pond

Sinkhole ponds and lakes have several unique aspects. If they form by intersecting the water table, they may connect through underwater passages to the aquifer, allowing the migration of aquatic species from lake to lake. These lakes and ponds may also come and go with the rise and fall of the water table, creating a temporary refuge for species that need water in which to breed.

When limestone dissolves in water, it has a buffering effect. It reduces the acidity of the water, which in turn attracts more specialized species of plants and aquatic life to a sinkhole pond. Some sinkhole ponds sparkle with a surreal bluish tint, the result of suspended limestone particles catching the sunlight.

Thanks to these special qualities, sinkhole ponds and lakes contribute to biodiversity. They provide a home for rare and endangered species of fish, reptiles, amphibians, and aquatic vegetation. Virginia sneezeweed, a rare herb, grows only in seasonally flooded sinkhole ponds in the Shenandoah Valley of Virginia. Chara, or stonewort, grows profusely in many sinkhole ponds, as it requires nutrients from limestone to flourish. Stonewort leaves are often encrusted with a film of limestone. In Missouri,

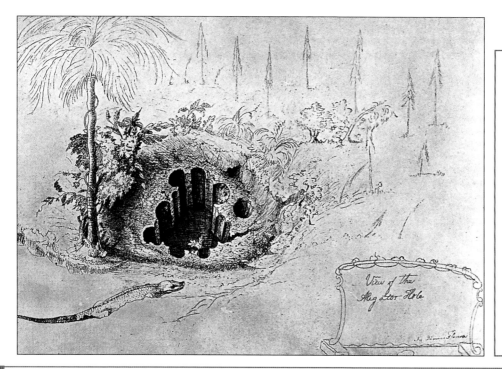

View of the Alligator Hole

When naturalist William Bartram passed through northern Florida in 1790, he saw alligators sunning themselves along sinkhole ponds. This is a sketch he made of a sinkhole near the ancient village of Talahasochte.
(Florida State Archives)

One of Virginia's many sinkhole ponds. (David A. Hubbard Jr., VDMME/DMR)

shallow, swampy Marg Pond supports four endangered plants, including manna grass. Rare longtail salamanders inhabit Glovers Pond in New Jersey, while tiger salamanders breed in Virginia's sinkhole ponds in early spring. Insects—especially dragonflies and praying mantises—are also attracted to sinkhole ponds.

A series of sinkholes near Paisley, Florida, serve as habitats for fish, turtles, and waterfowl. (Sandra Friend)

Living in a Spring

The headwaters of a first-magnitude spring teem with activity—bluegill darting in and out of the shallows, gar gliding smoothly below the surface, snails laying tracks across the glittering sands on the bottom, an alligator sunning on a log, a heron standing watch from a tree limb. Plants thrive around the water's edge; thick grasses carpet the bottom. Algae covers rocks, logs, and turtles.

At most springs, the water remains a constant temperature, unlike the water in a pond or a lake, which heats up during the day and cools down at night. In Florida, spring waters range between 66°F and 87°F, attracting creatures that need warmth to survive, especially ocean-going creatures that can tolerate fresh water. During the winter, manatees swim inland from their oceanic wandering to bask in the warm waters of Florida's springs, clustering near each spring's source. Winter temperatures also encourage saltwater fish such as sheepshead, mullet, gray snapper, and snook to gather en masse near the outflow of springs near the sea.

Other oceangoing creatures spend

A manatee floats through the shallows at Homosassa Springs. (Wendee and Matt Holtcamp)

Eels migrate inland to Juniper Springs in the Ocala National Forest in Florida to mature in the warm depths. (Sandra Friend)

a part of their life cycle in the spring. Born in the mysterious grassy portion of the Atlantic Ocean known as the Sargasso Sea, American eels make their way up rivers and streams to live out their lives near freshwater springs, only to return to the ocean to reproduce and die. Flounder start their lives hidden in the sandy bottoms of springs near the sea.

The spring environment attracts nonaquatic visitors as well. Mammals and rodents come to the water's edge to drink. Birds flock to the surrounding trees, where they can stand watch for a choice morsel floating below. But the fish have a fighting chance—most karst springs are so clear that the fish can see their predators.

Fresh- and saltwater fish cluster around the year-round warmth provided by the springs in Florida's Homosassa River. (Sandra Friend)

Cavern Dwellers

Sinkholes provide entryways to caverns, tempting animals to explore. Bats will discover any opening that leads them to a dark, cool roost underground, so sinkholes are important to the health of bat colonies. Bats provide a natural means of controlling the insect population, which in turn controls the spread of disease. A single little brown bat can eat more than 600 mosquitoes an hour. Some species of bats are essential in the pollination of certain plants, like peaches, bananas, and cashews.

Bats, crickets, mice, rats, and other part-time cavern dwellers come and go via sinkhole openings. These part-time visitors are called trogloxenes. Full-time cavern dwellers adapt to a life of total darkness. These animals, called troglobites, include the various blind or eyeless species of fish, snails,

A salamander on a cave wall.
(Jeremy Engle)

Pools of water deep within caverns may shimmer with the activity of cavefish and crayfish.
(Sandra Friend)

salamanders, crayfish, worms, beetles, and cave crickets. They cannot survive outside of the cave. Because of their lack of pigmentation, many of these creatures are white or almost clear in color.

A cave cricket.
(Jeremy Engle)

At the Oasis

In the desert, a sinkhole may provide the only access to fresh water hidden deep below the sands. The presence of a spring or an artesian well creates an oasis—a spot of green in an otherwise dry and lifeless terrain, a place where vegetation grows because of access to water. Since water is the central focus of the oasis, it becomes a gathering place for animals and humans. Archeological expeditions have discovered remnants of human habitation around well-established oases, since desert settlements were placed near these precious water sources. Trade routes through the desert ran from oasis to oasis to ensure both man and beast water at the end of a long day's walk.

Like sinkhole ponds, lakes, and springs, the sinkhole oasis supports a unique web of life. Unusual species thrive in and around the water. At Montezuma's Well in Arizona's Sonoran Desert, the sinkhole spring maintains a warm (75°F) temperature, inviting water scorpions to take up constant residence. Mesquite and ephedra are among the many plants that cluster along its steep-sided rim, forming the oasis. In the deserts of the Arabian Peninsula, especially in Jordan and Oman, oases attract endangered mammals, such as the

A village often springs up around a desert oasis. At Pushkar, this spring-fed sacred lake in India's Thar Desert attracts Hindu pilgrims from all over Asia. (Sandra Friend)

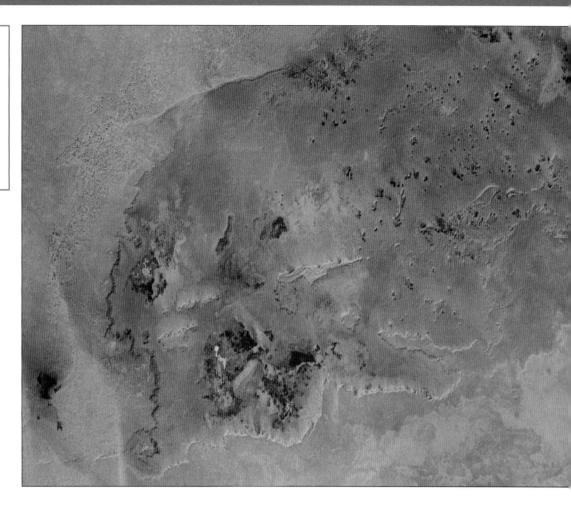

The springs of Siwa Oasis in Egypt, as photographed from the space shuttle. (NASA)

gazelle-like oryx and ibex. Seasonal wetlands that surround certain springs shelter thousands of migrating water birds. But these rare wetlands easily become threatened. The Al-Aflaj Lakes of Saudi Arabia, a group of more than 20 sinkholes forming an oasis wetland, supported a lush grassland until recent times. They now lie barren, their water pumped out for cattle to drink. As water continues to be drained from desert aquifers for agricultural use, the stability of the oasis ecosystem suffers.

In Ancient Times

Five thousand years ago, a busy trading center called Ubar dominated the Arabian Peninsula. Built at an oasis, the fortress city of Ubar attracted merchants from as far away as Greece thanks to its stock-in-trade: the leaves of the frankincense bush. Worth more than gold, they provided the sweet incense used in the ancient world's temples. Ubar prospered.

Suddenly Ubar disappeared. Legends said the people grew greedy and were destroyed by their god. Explorers attempted to find the city but failed. Even Lawrence of Arabia, who called Ubar the "Atlantis of the Sands," died without unlocking its secrets.

During the 1980s, researchers used sand-penetrating radar images from the space shuttle *Challenger* to guess where Ubar might be. NASA's Landsat satellite images helped them find the ancient trade routes, faint images in desert sands. In December 1991, an expedition arrived at Ash Shisur, Oman. They found a sinkhole and started to dig. As they uncovered the ruins of Ubar beneath the sands, the archeologists discovered why the city disappeared without a trace—a cavern roof had collapsed under Ubar, and it had fallen into a sinkhole.

Ancient peoples relied on sinkholes as a natural resource. Sinkholes provided fresh water for parched land, shelter from wind and rain, and fertile farmland. As evidenced by archeological finds in France and Ohio, sinkholes also provided "butcher shops" for Paleolithic peoples, who relied on these natural traps to capture animals for their meals. Discoveries of Ice Age arrowheads in Indiana show that Paleo-Indian peoples often lived on the shores of sinkhole ponds.

Sinkholes provided grist for myths and legends too. Australian aborigines shied away from "Undiri," the sinkholes in the Nullabor Plain, as they thought them gateways to the underworld, inhabited by evil spirits. The Mayan culture, on the other hand, built their cities around *cenotes*, which not only served as their water source but also played a part in their religious ceremonies.

The Sacred Well, a *cenote,* at Chichen Itza, Yucatan, Mexico. (Dave Bunnell)

Spotting a Sinkhole

Figuring out where sinkholes might develop takes some serious detective work. Fortunately, geologists and hydrologists have some excellent tools at their disposal, such

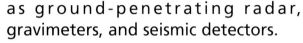

as ground-penetrating radar, gravimeters, and seismic detectors.

Ground-penetrating radar allows geologists to find sinkholes—even ancient ones—that have filled in with debris, mud, gravel, or sand. As an antenna is pulled or towed across the suspect ground, it radiates high-frequency electromagnetic waves. These waves respond to changes in the moisture content of the soil, the soil thickness, and the types of rocks under the surface. Once plotted into a rough map, the data gathered can help determine whether a sinkhole is underfoot.

Gravimeters measure tiny changes in gravity under the earth's surface. Wherever a cavity forms in karst, its gravity is slightly different than that of the surrounding rock. This difference allows geologists to measure and map cavities and fractures.

A sinkhole collapses for a second time, endangering the edge of a farmer's field in Shelby County, Alabama. (Geological Survey of Alabama)

The circular cracking of Big Sink in Shelby County, Alabama, carried large trees, intact, into the sinkhole.
(Paul Moser, Geological Survey of Alabama)

From tremors caused by heavy equipment to those created by large earthquakes, seismic detectors measure movements under the earth's surface. Their readings allow geologists to determine whether karst is unstable due to cavern collapse deep below the surface.

Even without high-tech tools, you can follow these four simple steps to determine if a sinkhole is forming:

1. Research the geology of the area. Is it karst?
2. Inspect the ground carefully for signs of subsidence.
3. Look for circular or linear cracks in the soil.
4. Look for signs that vegetation has been stressed. Are plants dying?

If any of these signs are present, call your state geologic survey office so a geologist can verify your findings and you can take action.

When the Earth Yawns

Just like a tornado, a sinkhole can strike suddenly and unexpectedly, causing random and extensive damage to property and putting people's lives in danger. The rapid appearance of a sinkhole can rupture gas, water, and sewer pipelines, disrupt electrical service, divert drainage, crack the foundation of a building, or even swallow whole buildings. While it's rare that a sinkhole will happen without some warning, what do you do when a sinkhole opens?

If you see a sinkhole open up in a highway, immediately call the police to report it. Authorities will need to set up a barricade around the hole and perhaps close the road down while repairs are being made. A sinkhole in a highway can have deadly results for the driver of the first car that drops a wheel into the hole. Even if the sinkhole is on the shoulder of the road, you should report it to the police, since the sinkhole could spread into the highway.

If a sinkhole opens up in your yard, placement is everything. Where is it? How quickly did it appear? Are there numerous fresh cracks in the earth

Surrounded by thousands of other houses in a suburban Orlando neighborhood, this house was the unlucky one—a sinkhole opened up under the living room floor. As the sinkhole grew, the house collapsed inward into the hole. The family quickly evacuated, and the house was later demolished. (Sandra Friend)

In 1963, this Bartow, Florida, home slid into a giant sinkhole. (Florida Geological Survey Collection,

around it? If the sinkhole is anywhere near or under the foundation of your home, you'll need to evacuate the area until the sinkhole is stabilized. If the collapse was sudden or large, contact your local fire department or police department for instructions on how to proceed.

If the sinkhole in your yard is small and not an immediate threat, secure the area by placing barriers or bright tape around it. If you can, cover it with boards to keep out children and animals. Do not allow anyone to climb down into the sinkhole, as the earth can be extremely unstable and unsafe. Report the problem to your insurance company. If you live in a karst area, you should maintain coverage for sinkhole damage.

If you see a new sinkhole on undeveloped land, pass the word along to your state or regional geologic survey office so someone can investigate the situation.

Sinkhole collapse on level ground near a home. (Samuel S. Frushour, Indiana Geological Survey)

Filling a Sinkhole

Dumping soil, mud, and concrete into a sinkhole isn't going to permanently prevent that sinkhole from opening up again. But when a sinkhole opens up under a building or in a road, it must be filled. The process of intentionally filling and covering a sinkhole is called remediation.

The most popular sinkhole-filling material is clay. It provides a barrier against water flowing into the sinkhole but allows some water to trickle through. A mixture of large stones and concrete may provide stability, but water will eventually erode the edges of the plug. Since sinkholes funnel water, care must be taken to avoid plugging up sinkholes that provide critical recharge to the water table. If the sinkhole must be filled due to its location, a mixture of loose gravel and crushed stone allows water to continue seeping into the sinkhole, much like a French drain.

Some engineers use special grouting, similar to the grout around a bathtub. Sodium silicate grout mixes with the soil to create a sandstone-like mass. Using pipes driven into the ground surrounding a sinkhole, engineers inject the grout mixture into the sinkhole under high pressure to seal the cavities in the karst. After the bedrock is stable, grouting continues

Excavating sinkholes can be an eye-opening process: like an iceberg, you never know how much is below the surface. When a developer decided to put houses in this sinkhole-prone area near Lexington, Kentucky, local regulations made it necessary for him to excavate and remediate existing sinkholes. (James R. Rebmann, Photographer)

After the smallest sinkhole was excavated as a trench, it was lined with filter fabric and loose stones. (James R. Rebmann, Photographer)

as the pipes are removed, allowing the loose soils inside and around the sinkhole to stabilize.

The best long-term way to fill and stabilize a sinkhole is to first excavate the sinkhole down to the bedrock. It should then be filled with a progression of material from coarse to fine, the material getting finer as the top of the sinkhole is reached. A concrete cap is then put on the top.

The largest sinkhole in the group was nearly 150 feet long. Because of its size, workers laid rebar (reinforcing steel bars) and poured a concrete foundation in the sinkhole, leaving drainage holes so water flow would not be restricted. Above this, a layer of filter fabric was covered with loose stone and the excavation backfilled with soil before construction began. (James R. Rebmann, Photographer)

Careful Construction

When planning construction in karst terrain, engineers and architects must carefully place buildings and roads, since construction in karst can trigger any of the three types of sinkholes. Structural engineers, concerned with making sure buildings are structurally sound, must plan for the possibility of sinkholes. A sinkhole opening up under a building can cause cracks in the foundation or can cause the building to slide right off its foundation.

Placing utilities underground often triggers sinkholes. Shelby County in Alabama has suffered numerous sinkholes linked to pipeline placement, including the enormous "December Giant" of 1972. The weight of a pipeline, with its ebb and flow of fluid pressure, adds stress to weak karst. In gypsum karst, particularly, the slightest amount of extra weight can make a big difference. Sinkholes tend to form along highways, railroad tracks, electric lines, oil pipes—anything linear than puts pressure on the fragile gypsum karst. These buried linear features allow water in the ground to move along them, promoting later collapse.

Before building in karst, the ground must be tested. Can it handle the weight of construction? Are there cavities below the site, and should they be filled? Engineers and geologists must find the answers. Sometimes depressions in the bedrock can be filled with grout to add to the stability of

Remediation of a sinkhole along I-81 in Virginia. (David A. Hubbard Jr., VDMME/DMR)

Homes built within a broad sinkhole. The rear yard of one home has sinkhole ponds, which pose a health hazard. Building foundations may settle when buildings are improperly located within a sinkhole. (Samuel S. Frushour, Indiana Geological Survey)

the land. In other areas, foundations must be laid on top of pillars of concrete that extend deep into the bedrock. Construction sites are most vulnerable to sinkhole formation while construction is going on.

This sinkhole collapse endangers a water line. The sinkhole filled with soil the water line was installed, but runoff from precipitation and the infiltration of moisture reopened the sinkhole. (Samuel S. Frushour, Indiana Geological Survey)

Guarding Against Collapse

How can we avoid creating more sinkholes? Since heavy construction can trigger sinkholes, urban development in karst areas makes the sinkhole problem worse. When trees are clear-cut from a property in preparation for construction, the protective layer of roots and soil are removed from the bedrock, leaving it vulnerable to erosion. Grading the land removes more soil from some spots and piles it higher in others, a sure recipe for sand and soil to trickle down into the karst. Grading also changes the dynamics of water flow across the land, further encouraging erosion. The sonic vibrations created by heavy construction equipment can loosen weak rock, encouraging a cavern roof collapse. The removal of a large boulder or shock waves from blasting can also cause sudden collapse.

Developers must plan carefully when they build in areas vulnerable to sinkhole formation. To guard against collapse, construction techniques must take into account the nature of karst terrain. The flow of water across the landscape is as important as the landscape itself. One of the worst mistakes people make is to drain stormwater runoff into a sinkhole. Not only does it contaminate the water supply, but adding excessive water to a sinkhole can also kick off a chain reaction in which many more sinkholes open up.

Sinkhole collapse endangering a home in Indiana (Samuel S. Frushour, Indiana Geological Survey)

Retention ponds in karst areas must be carefully planned. Not long after its creation, this retention pond in Ocala, Florida, developed subsidence sinkholes after the first major rainstorm. (Kelly Lyn Friend)

Nature's Bounty

Thanks to sinkholes, Slovenia's poljes have traditionally provided the best farmland in this rocky, dry mountain region. The rest of the country is too dry to support farming, but in the poljes, farmers grow potatoes, wheat, and hay despite the possibility of flooding. In Jamaica, farmers grow bananas, yams, corn, and sugar cane in banana holes. They rely on the rich dirt at the bottom of these old sinkholes to nourish their crops. Banana holes are generally oval in shape and often ten to twelve feet deep. As collapse sinkholes, they are prone to further collapse but indispensable as good farmland. Indonesians line their giant sinkholes with terraces to support rice paddies, corn, and cassava. Settlers in the Florida Keys once used sinkholes for farming as well, planting crops in small solution sinkholes they dubbed kettle holes.

But farming in sinkhole regions can be problematic. In Japan, many sinkholes are filled in with good soil to provide spots for sugar cane to grow. These crops often struggle, however, since fertilizers and water seep out through the sinkhole's bottom. Further, livestock and sinkholes don't always mix. Unless a deep sinkhole is fenced off, cattle, sheep, and horses may slip and fall into the hole, suffering a fatal injury.

Cows meander through a Kentucky pasture, its rolling hills and valleys a landscape of solution sinkholes. (Deanna Davis, Kentucky Geological Survey)

A polje in Yugoslavia. (David A. Hubbard Jr.)

This 1918 photo shows a banana plant flourishing along with other tropical plants in the depths of a sinkhole in Citrus County, Florida. (John Kunkel Small, Florida State Archives)

Buried Treasure

Many of the earth's sinkholes have been around for hundreds, thousands, even millions of years. Hidden in forests and fields, some of these old, stable sinkholes filled back up with mud and sand, covering buried treasure of various kinds.

Archeologists continue to unearth amazing finds inside soil- and water-filled sinkholes. Some filled sinkholes in the Midwest contain important metals, like zinc and lead. A sinkhole near Carey, Ohio, yielded bones from more than 60 Ice Age animal species butchered by Paleolithic peoples, whose spear points, scrapers, and tools were also found inside the sinkhole.

Underwater archeologists in Florida have been working since 1983 inside a sinkhole called Little Salt Spring, located between Fort Myers and Sarasota, where they've discovered human remains more than 7,000 years old and tools thought to be up to 12,000 years old. The water's unique chemistry—brackish and lacking oxygen—is thought to have per-fectly preserved these artifacts. Another exciting project continues in the Dominican Republic, where researchers from Indiana University are diving into El Manantial de la Aleta, a deep, bell-shaped sinkhole with a narrow entrance, and finding artifacts from the Taino culture. The Taino people perished in a war with the Spaniards in 1503, but discovery of their pottery and food vessels at the bottom of this 115-foot-deep sinkhole is helping unlock the mysteries of their culture.

In 1778, miners came to Sinking Valley, Pennsylvania. Looking for critical supplies of lead ore they established Fort Roberdeau to protect the mining camp. Sinkholes are very common in Sinking Valley, and many are old enough to have baffled researchers trying to determine the original location of the Colonial-era lead mines. Was galena initially exposed and discovered due to the sinkholes, or are some of the sinkholes actually mine pits?

A reconstruction of Fort Roberdeau, east of Altoona, Pennsylvania. (Sandra Friend)

Galena crystals. (Sandra Friend)

Fort Roberdeau, Sinking Valley, Pennsylvania, as depicted in *Columbian* magazine, 1788 (Fort Roberdeau archives)

One Big Toilet

In 1916, genteel tourists visited Kentucky's picturesque Hidden River Cave by boat. The townspeople of Hidden River tapped the river for drinking water—and dumped their raw sewage into the numerous sinkholes around the town. By the mid 1930s, they could no longer drink the water. By the 1940s, boat rides into the cave were stopped because the cave smelled like a toilet. It had, in effect, become the town's sewer. All life within the cave died.

Unlike aquifers of sand and gravel, which filter groundwater, karst aquifers easily fill with pollutants. In the 1890s, French speleologist Edouard-Alfred Martel discovered that groundwater in karst regions carried bacteria and viruses over vast areas. He worked to ban the dumping of garbage and animal carcasses into sinkholes. Today, we still experience problems with garbage being dumped into sinkholes, and we need to inform farmers that manure should not be spread near a sinkhole. Both can have a devastating effect on the water supply.

In the early 1800s, settlers near St. Louis in the Louisiana Territory experienced the deadly consequences of their lack of understanding of how water flowed through karst. The waste from their barnyards and privies soaked directly down into the karst. Water taken from deep, new wells started to kill livestock. Babies were born with blue skin. The culprit was nitrate poisoning, caused by high levels of fecal matter contaminating their water.

People who live in sinkhole-prone areas may also experience problems with toxic fumes. Leaking gas tanks at abandoned gas stations, chemical spills, and deliberate dumping of toxins into sinkholes can create a witch's brew of chemicals underground, generating toxic fumes. The fumes may be trapped deep in the earth for months, even years, before they start seeping into people's basements, pushed upward by a rising water table.

Damage to karst waters can sometimes be repaired. Thanks to conservation efforts in recent decades, fresh water again flows through Hidden River Cave and the aquatic life has returned.

Sinkhole dumping in central Florida. Garbage fills this roadside sinkhole, and the reek of dead animals rises from the hole. (Sandra Friend)

A problematic location for a fresh sinkhole—a sewage lagoon in Centerville, Alabama. (Paul Moser, Geological Survey of Alabama)

Water: A Precious Resource

With pollutants being dumped into sinkholes, it's a challenge to keep water fresh and clean in karst. To determine how water flows through karst, hydrologists use a special technique called dye tracing. This involves pouring a detectable dye, such as potassium chloride or sodium chloride, into the water and tracking its route as it vanishes into swallow holes and reappears through springs. The first such experiments were done along the Danube River in 1878. Using these techniques, hydrologists can learn how far water travels from the entry point into the karst (typically a sinkhole) to its exit point (a spring or well). This allows them to pinpoint problems with pollutants.

Another great challenge to karst waters is the pumping of too much fresh water from a karst aquifer near the ocean, usually due to heavy development along a coastline. When the water table drops, the sea pushes inland underground. This results in undrinkable water. Saltwater intrusion is a serious problem for coastal cities around the globe. Puerto Rico suffers from saltwater intrusion and high levels of nitrates and chlorides in its karst. In the Yucatan Peninsula of Mexico, inlets called *caletas* mix fresh water with seawater. The *cenotes* of the Yucatan, the only fresh water

A researcher introduces non-toxic water tracing dye into a sinking stream in Bourbon County, Kentucky. The springs where the dye might reappear will be monitored to map karst groundwater flow. (Jim Currens, Lexington, KY)

Dumping trash into sinkholes causes contamination of the water supply, especially when detergents are dumped.
(Samuel S. Frushour, Indiana Geological Survey)

source for the region, form along fractures in the limestone leading away from *caletas.* When the water table drops due to drought, the *cenotes* suffer saltwater intrusion.

Florida's coastal aquifers play a constant tug of war with the ocean. In heavily populated areas, the use of water from the aquifer almost always exceeds the amount of water recharging the system. Droughts and development of open areas where rainfall used to recharge the karst add to the problem.

One method of fighting saltwater intrusion is to create barrier wells near the coastline. These wells pump out the sea, preventing it from seeping further inland. But a practical, long-term plan involves much more: limits on groundwater use and promotion of freshwater conservation. The Georgia Environmental Protection Division developed such a plan to prevent saltwater contamination of wells in Savannah, Brunswick, and the barrier islands. Only with these steps can coastal cities ensure adequate supplies of drinking water.

Save That Sinkhole!

Will a sinkhole ever affect you? Possibly, but not in the dramatic way you see on television. If you live in a karst region, sinkholes will affect you by the role they play in your water supply. Are people dumping old tires and washing machines into sinkholes? Are farmers spreading manure too close to sinkholes? If so, your water may be polluted by this waste. Work with local authorities to clean out sinkhole dumps. Develop local ordinances to ensure that proper construction techniques are used near sinkholes so more sinkholes don't occur. Through your efforts, your drinking water will stay fresh and clean.

In wilderness areas, protecting sinkhole habitats means proper management of the surrounding land. When trees are cut down, erosion happens more rapidly. Existing sinkholes become filled with debris and soil. The karst becomes more prone to ravelling and more likely to collapse. Clear-cutting of trees causes permanent ecological damage. Since soil washes away so quickly from bare karst, erosion strikes a deathblow to the ecosystem. Without soil, plants will not return; without plants, the barren karst continues to erode, creating a rocky landscape unable to support life.

Trash dumped into sinkholes may disappear from the surface, but it doesn't go away. It moves into caves and underground streams.
(Jim Currens, Lexington, KY)

Rugged karst mountaintop on the island of Corfu, Greece. The clearing of forests in Greece began thousands of years ago, causing the destruction of lush ecosystems. People fought over the control of sinkholes and swallow holes in the Pelopennese since they provided agriculture with much-needed water. But now the trees are gone—and much of Greece is barren, rocky karst. (Sandra Friend)

To conserve endangered bat populations, it's important to keep sinkhole entrances to known bat-nesting caves free and clear of debris. In the case of one Kentucky sinkhole that led to a bat cave, the population of endangered gray bats grew from only 1 in 1999 to 400 a year later. Bats returned to the cave from other places after the sinkhole had been cleared of trailerloads of garbage and loose rocks.

Many groups are willing and able to help clean up sinkholes. Do you know of a contaminated or garbage-filled sinkhole near you? Contact your state's department of natural resources, your local soil and water conservation district, the U.S. Fish and Wildlife Service, or the local chapter of the National Speleological Society. These are all organizations that care about the impact of trash in sinkholes.

Trash dumping in a sinkhole in Sylacauga, Alabama. (Geological Survey of Alabama)

A Natural Wonder

Sinkholes provide many opportunities for outdoor recreation. Fishermen and boaters enjoy relaxing days out on the waters of sinkhole lakes. Swimmers of all ages flock to springs to bask in the clear, deep water that remains a constant temperature. Cavers seek out sinkholes as potential entrances to caverns, enjoying a scramble in the depths of the earth. Hikers walk along sinkhole trails, following paths around massive sinkholes. Tourists of all types stop and pause at the curious natural wonder that a sinkhole provides.

Cave divers use sinkholes to explore the interconnections between sinkholes and the aquifer. They often uncover amazing finds including the fossilized remains of animals that fell into a sinkhole in prehistoric times. Diving 200 feet down into Wakulla Springs, divers found the bones of deer, giant sloths, and mastodons. At Silver Springs, cave divers found the bones and teeth of a mastodon, carbon-dated to be more than 10,000 years old.

Parks around the globe feature sinkholes and karst as part of their landscape, and sometimes a single sinkhole is the main attraction. The possibilities are endless. Take the time to ponder one of nature's oddities: visit a sinkhole near you.

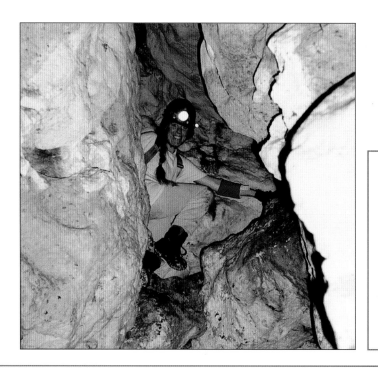

Caver Caren Beck climbs up into a sinkhole entrance in central Florida's Jennings Cave.
(Sandra Friend)

Turn-of-the-century tourists considered the Devil's Millhopper in Gainesville, Florida, a must-see attraction. (P. K. Yonge Library of Florida History)

Cave divers prepare to enter Blue Spring in Deland, Florida. (Sandra Friend)

This trail leads into the Ocala National Forest for an up-close look at the Lake Eaton Sinkhole. A boardwalk goes to the sinkhole's bottom. (Sandra Friend)

Hiker Linda Patton pauses along a segment of the Florida National Scenic Trail following the Aucilla River Sinks. Sinkholes dominate the course of the river as it pops in and out of porous karst on its way to the Gulf of Mexico. (Sandra Friend)

Where to Visit a Sinkhole

Thousands of sinkholes dot our public lands, hidden away in forests, national parks, state parks, and even local parks that protect karst formations. Use this list as a starting point for your own geologic explorations.

Alabama
Blue Lake (Conecuh National Forest)
Blue Springs State Park (Clio)

Arizona
Karchner Caverns State Park (Cochise County)
Montezuma Well National Monument (Upper Sonoran Desert)

California
Gray Whale Ranch State Park (Santa Cruz)
Salton Sea State Recreation Area (North Shore)

Florida
Aucilla Sinks (Florida National Scenic Trail, St. Marks)
Citrus Tract (Withlacoochee State Forest, Ridge Manor)
Devil's Millhopper State Geologic Site (Gainesville)
Everglades National Park
Falling Waters State Reserve (Chipley)
Florida Caverns State Park (Marianna)
Hidden Waters Reserve (Eustis)
Hillsborough River State Park (Thontonassa)
Kanapaha Botanical Gardens (Gainesville)
Lake Eaton Sinkhole (Ocala National Forest)
Leon Sinks Geologic Area (Woodville)
O'Leno State Park (High Springs)
Peacock Springs State Recreation Area (Live Oak)
Ravine Gardens (Palatka)
Richloam Tract (Withlacoochee State Forest, Ridge Manor)
San Felasco State Reserve (Gainesville)
Scott Spring (Ocala)
Silver River State Park (Silver Springs)
Wekiva Springs State Park (Orlando)
Windley Key Fossil Reef State Geologic Site (Windley Key)

Illinois
Mississippi Palisades State Park (Savanna)

Indiana
Charlestown State Park (Charlestown)
Spring Mill State Park (Mitchell)

Kentucky
Big Bone Lick State Park (Union)
Hidden River Cave (Horse Cave)
Hundred Acre Pond (Monroe)
Mammoth Cave National Park (Mammoth Cave)

Michigan
The Sinkholes Pathway (Onaway)

Missouri

32-Rock Bridge Memorial State Park (Columbia)
Cuivre River State Park (Troy)
Grand Gulf State Park (Thayer)
Grassy Pond (Peck Ranch Conservation Area, Winona)
Ha Ha Tonka State Park (Camdenton)
Lily Pond Natural Area (Redford)
Marg Pond Natural Area (Mark Twain National Forest)
Meramec State Park (Sullivan)
Ozark National Scenic River (Van Buren)
Pioneer Forest (Salem)
Rock Bridge Memorial State Park (Columbia)

Montana

Lost Water Canyon (Custer National Forest)
Pryor Mountain Wild Horse Territory (Red Lodge)

New Jersey

Glovers Pond Preserve (Johnsonburg)
Swartswood State Park (Newton)

New Mexico

Bottomless Lakes State Park (Roswell)
Carlsbad Caverns National Park (Carlsbad)

Oklahoma

Alabaster Caverns State Park (Freedom)

Pennsylvania

Fort Roberdeau (Blair County)
Lincoln Caverns (Huntington)
The Link Trail (Mapleton)
Penn's Cave (Centre Hall)

South Carolina

Santee State Park (Santee)

South Dakota

The Mammoth Site (Hot Springs)

Tennessee

Cades Cove (Great Smoky Mountains National Park)
Ijams Nature Center (Knoxville)

Texas

Devil's Sinkhole State Natural Area (Brackettville)

Utah

Gypsum Sinkhole (Capitol Reef National Park)

Virginia

Endless Caverns (New Market)
Grand Caverns (Grottoes)
Natural Bridge (Natural Bridge)

West Virginia

Yankauer Nature Preserve (Shepherdstown)

Canada

Bruce Peninsula National Park (Ontario)
Wood Buffalo National Park (Alberta)

Additional Resources

Information for this book was complied from an extensive variety of sources, including books, websites, technical journals, and newspaper articles. The following books provide in-depth and frequently technical information on sinkholes and karst.

Beck, Barry, ed. *Karst Geohazards: Engineering and Environmental Problems in Karst Terrane.* Boston: A. A. Balkema, 1995.

Beck, Barry F., ed. *Sinkholes: Their Geology, Engineering, and Environmental Impact.* Boston: A. A. Balkema, 1984.

Drew, David. *Karst Processes and Landforms.* London: MacMillan Education, 1985.

Ford, Derek C., and Paul Williams. *Karst Geomorphology and Hydrology.* Winchester, MA: Unwin Hyman, 1989.

Herak, M., and V. T. Stringfield, eds. *Important Karst Regions of the Northern Hemisphere.* New York: Elsevier Publishing, 1972.

Jakucs, Lazlo. *Morphogenetics of Karst Regions.* Bristol, England: Adam Hilger, Ltd., 1977.

Jennings, J. N. *Karst Geomorphology.* New York: Basil Blackwell, Inc., 1985.

Klimchouk, A. B., et al. *Speleogenesis: Evolution of Karst Aquifers.* Huntsville, AL: National Speleological Society, 2000.

Larousse Encyclopedia of the Earth. England: Paul Hamlyn, Ltd., 1961.

Sweeting, Marjorie M. *Karst Landforms.* New York: Columbia University Press, 1973.

Trudgill, Stephen. *Limestone Geomorphology.* New York: Longman Group Ltd., 1985.

White, William B. *Geomorphology and Hydrology of Karst Terrains.* New York: Oxford University Press, 1988.

Williams, Paul W., ed. *Karst Terrains: Environmental Changes and Human Impact.* Cremlingen-Destedt, Germany: Catena Verlag, 1993.

Wycoff, Jerome. *Rock, Time, and Landforms.* New York: Harper and Row, 1966.

Less technical in nature, these books provide general information about sinkholes, caverns, and karst.

Erickson, Jon. *The Changing Earth: Quakes, Eruptions, and Other Geologic Cataclysms.* New York: Facts on File, Inc., 1994.

Erickson, Jon. *Craters, Caverns, and Canyons: Delving Beneath the Earth's Surface.* New York: Facts on File, Inc., 1993.

Harrison, David L. *The World of American Caves.* Chicago: Reilly & Lee Books, 1970.

Jackson, Donald Dale. *Planet Earth: Underground Worlds.* Alexandria, VA: Time-Life Books, 1982.

Lambert, David. *The Field Guide to Geology.* New York: Facts on File, Inc., 1988.

Moore, George W., and G. Nicolas Sullivan. *Speleology: The Study of Caves.* St. Louis, MO: Cave Books, 1978.

Tufty, Barbara. *1001 Questions Answered About Natural Land Disasters.* New York: Dodd, Mead, and Company, 1969.

Veni, G., et al. *Living with Karst: A Fragile Foundation.* Arlington, VA: American Geological Institute, 2001.

Zokaites, Carol, ed. *Living on Karst: A Reference Guide for Landowners in Limestone Regions.* Glen Allen, VA: Cave Conservancy of the Virginias, 1997.

Geological Survey websites are treasure troves of information about sinkholes in your region. Many states and provinces offer booklets and educational materials on sinkholes.

People with an interest in the unusual geology of karst may want to join the National Speleological Society. The organization focuses on cave conservation and the study of caves and karst features. It produces an excellent monthly magazine, the *NSS News*, and a quarterly publication, the *Journal of Cave and Karst Studies.* Write to National Speleological Society, 2813 Cave Avenue, Huntsville AL 35810-4431 or visit their web site at www.caves.org.

Glossary

aquifer – an underground water reservoir

aquitard – an obstruction that stops water flow

artesian well – a well in which pressure from the aquifer below pushes the water up above the level to which the well was dug

banana hole – a collapse sinkhole into a shallow cave, usually found in tropical regions

barrier well – a well used to pump out seawater to prevent saltwater intrusion into an aquifer

bedrock – solid rock exposed on the earth's surface

biodiversity – the existence of a wide variety of species in a particular area

blind valley – a karst valley that ends abruptly where a stream disappears underground

blue hole – a solution sinkhole in the bottom of the ocean; a sinkhole spring where water rises with a bluish tint caused by dissolved limestone

caleta – ocean inlet in the Yucatan Peninsula of Mexico

cave – a natural open area under the ground, caused by erosion or dissolution of rock

cave diver – a person who uses special scuba gear to explore water-filled caves

caver – a person who makes a hobby of exploring and studying caves

cenote – water-filled sinkhole in the Yucatan Peninsula of Mexico that intersects the Yucatan Aquifer

cockpit karst – rounded, gumdrop-shaped karst hills found primarily in the tropics

corrosion – the gradual process of chemicals deteriorating rock

deposition – the deposit of any material by any natural process

dewatering – the pumping of water out of a mine to keep the mine tunnels dry

dissolution – the process of dissolving

doline – the international term for sinkhole; often used to refer to broad, shallow, bowl-shaped sinkholes

dry valley – a valley in karst terrain without a surface flow of water

dye tracing – a technique used to determine where water flows by adding a known quantity of dye and searching for where it ends up and in what concentration

epikarst – the top layer of karst bedrock, often exposed to the elements

estavelle – a sinkhole that reverses water flow

groundwater – water existing and/or flowing beneath the surface of the earth

haystack hill – a perfectly rounded hill formed by karst erosion, typically in the tropics

hydrologic – involving water

hydrologist – a scientist who studies the existence and flow of water

joint – a natural linear crack between two pieces of rock that used to be a single slab of rock

karren – small karst formations created by surface dissolution of the bedrock

karst – collectively, all landforms created primarily by the dissolution of rock by natural waters

karst window – a downward opening into karst showing a stream flowing below

kettle hole – a small, bowl-shaped depression

limestone – a sedimentary rock primarily formed from the remains of sea creatures and maritime ooze

littoral – the shoreline area between low and high tide

losing stream – a stream that seeps down into its karst bed until it finally disappears

microclimate – the climate that forms in a confined area, such as a sinkhole or cavern

mogote – rounded hill created by erosion of karst, usually found in tropical regions

natural bridge – a rock bridge formed by erosion or dissolution

oasis – a spring in the desert

pavement – a bare, flat karst surface broken into blocks by joints widened by dissolution

pepino – a rounded hill created by dissolution, usually found in tropical regions

permeability – the ability of soil or rock to absorb water

phreate – the zone of groundwater where water fills all the voids; the saturated zone below the water table; also called saturation zone

pocket valley – a valley that opens up from a large spring

polje – a low, broad depression draining underground

ponor – a swallow hole through which water passes to or from an underground passage

pseudokarst – terrain with landforms that look like the product of dissolution but that formed through other processes

ravelling – the particle-by-particle movement of soil down into cavities in the rock below

recharge – the movement of water into an aquifer

remediation – the process of filling a sinkhole properly so it doesn't reopen

resurgence – a spring that brings water back to the surface after the water has flowed into a swallow hole on higher ground

saturation zone – the zone of groundwater where water fills all the voids; the saturated zone below the water table; also called phreate

sink – a place where a stream or river disappears underground; also called riversink

sinkhole – a closed depression on the surface of the earth, formed by dissolution of the bedrock beneath and the downward movement of material into cavities or fractures

solution hole – a sinkhole that forms through gradual dissolution rather than collapse

solution pan – a broad, shallow depression in karst

solution pipe – a vertical, pipe-shaped shaft formed by gradual dissolution of karst

speleologist – a scientist who studies caves

spring – a natural flow of water out of the ground onto the surface of the earth

subsidence – the downward movement of soil and rock into cavities in the earth

swallow hole – a sinkhole that swallows a flowing body of water

thermokarst – an irregular, karstlike landscape caused by the melting of permafrost

tower karst – steep, rounded mountains formed by erosion of a karst plain

troglobite – a creature that can survive only inside a cave

troglophile – a creature that prefers to live inside a cave

trogloxene – a creature that lives mostly outside caves but used caves for shelter and food

uvala – a depression created when two or more sinkholes join together

water table – the level at which water completely fills the rock below it; the plane of separation between the vadose and phreate zones of groundwater

vadose – the zone of groundwater where not all voids are filled with water; the unsaturated zone above the water table

Index

Page numbers in *italics* refer to illustrations.

Acidity, 12, 16, 24, 26, 41, 56
Adriatic Sea, 12, 31, 36, 52
Africa, 6, 43
agriculture, 44, 63–64, 66, 76–77, 80, 85
Alabama, 5, 9, 12, 21, 46, 66–67, 72, 81, 85
Alachua Sink, 34
Al-Aflaj, Saudia Arabia, 63
Alaska, 6
alkaline, 54
Allegheny Mountains, 31
alligator, *34, 56,* 58
Altoona, PA, 79
American eel, 59
American hart's tongue fern, 54
Anastasia Island, FL, 53
Apalachicola Bay, 53
Apalachicola River, 40
Appalachian Mountains, 13, 31, 55
aquifer, 46, *47,* 50, 52, 56, 63, 80, 82–83, 86
aquitard, 30
Arabian Desert, 6, 48
Arabian Peninsula, 62, 64
Aradus, Italy, 52
aragonite, *27*
archeology, 9, 62, 64, 78
Arizona, 62
arrowhead, 64, 78
artesian, *48–49,* 51–52, 62
Artois, France, 48
Ash Shishur, Oman, 64
Atlantic Ocean, 36, 59
Aucilla River, *87*
Austin, TX, 46
Australia, 6, 36, 64
Bahamas, 36–37, 52
Bahrain, 52
banana hole, 76
banana, 60, 76–77
Barbados, 52
barrier well, 83
Bartow, FL, 69
Bartram, William, 56
basalt, 18
bat, 9, 25, 60, 85
bear, 54
bedding plane, 14
bedrock, 12, 14–16, 18, 20, 22–24, 26, 40, 46, 50, 70–73
beetle, 54, 60
Belize, 6, 37
Beruit, Lebanon, 48
Bikini Island, 36
biodiversity, 5, 6, 9
biologist, 9
Biscayne Aquifer, 46
blind valley, 30
blue hole, *36–37,* 52

Blue Hole, Belize, *37*
Blue Spring, 87
bluegill, 58
bone, 8, 14, 78, 86
Bourbon County, KY, 82
brachiopod, 14
Brunswick, GA, 83
Calcite, 14, *26,* 26–27
calcium, 14
caleta, 82, 83
California, 6, 10–11, 52
canyon, 31
carbon dioxide, 16, 24, 26
Carey, Ohio, 78
Carlsbad Caverns, 24
Carus, Titus Lucretius, 52
cashew, 60
Cass Cave, 32
cassava, 76
cattle, 63, 76
cave bacon, *26*
cave diver, 46–47, *47,* 53, 86–87, *87*
cave formation, *26–27*
Cave River, 44
cave, 4–5, 7, 9, 12–13, 15, *18–19, 21, 24–32,* 42, *44–48,* 50, 54, 60–61, *61,* 64, 67, 74, 80, *84,* 86
caver, 7, 24, *86*
cavern, 4–5, 7, 9, 12–13, 15, *18–19, 21, 24–32,* 42, *44–48,* 50, 54, 60–61, *61,* 64, 67, 74, 80, *84,* 86
cavity, 15, 18, 22, 66, 70, 72
Cedar Key, FL, 52, 53
cenote, 46, 64, *65,* 82, 83
Centreville, AL, 81
chalk, 14
chara, 56
Chichen Itza, Mexico, 65
China, 28–29
Chipola River, *33*
chloride, 82
Choctawhatchee River, 53
Citrus County, FL, 19, 77
Civil War, 33
clay, 13, 20, 70
cockpit karst, 28
collapse, 4, 6, 8, 10–11, 15, 18–22, 38, 42–43, 54–55, 64, 66–69, 73–74, 84
concrete, 4, 16, 70–71, 73
conservation, 9, 80, 83, 85
construction, 9, 20, 38, 42, 70–74
coral, 6, 14
Corfu, Greece, 14, *85*
corn, 76
corrosion, 16
crayfish, 54, 60–61
Crescent Beach Submarine Spring, 53
Crescent Beach, FL, 53
cricket, *60*
crops grown in sinkholes, 76–77
Danube River, 82
Deland, FL, 87

deposition, 26
desert, 6, 46, 48, 62–64
Devil's Millhopper, *55, 87*
Devil's River limestone, 19
dewatering, 43
dissolution, 15–16, 18, 24, 26, 28–29, 41
dolina, 16–17, *17*
doline, 16–17, *17*
dolostone, 14
Dominican Republic, 78
Donaldson Cave, *45*
dragonfly, 57
dry valley, 30
dumping, *80–85*
dye tracing, *82*
Earthquake, 11, 67
Edwards Aquifer, 46
Egypt, 63
engineer, 8, 72
England (*see* Great Britain)
Eocene, 36
ephedra, 62
epikarst, 12, 16
erosion, 11, 12, *14,* 15, 18, 22, 28, 42, 74, 84
estavelle, 35
Fell Beck, Great Britain, 32
fern, 54–55
fish, 52, 56–57, 59, 60–61
flooding, 18, 41, 44–46, 76
Florida Caverns State Park, *24, 27, 33, 49*
Florida Keys, 36, 76
Florida, 18, 46, 50–51, 54, 83
Floridan Aquifer, 46–47
flounder, 59
flowstone, *26–27*
fluid pressure, 10, 72
Fort Myers, FL, 78
Fort Roberdeau, PA, 78–79, *79*
fossil, 14, 38, 86
fox, 55
France, *13,* 48, 64, 80
frankincense, 64
French Pyrenees, 13
Gainesville, FL, 34, 42, 44, 55, 87
galena, 78, *79*
Galveston, TX, 10
Gaping Ghyll, 32
gar, 58
geologist, *8–9,* 38, 66–67, 72
Georgia, 46, 83
Germany, 6, 40
Glovers Pond, NJ, 57
gorge, 31
gravel, 38, 46, 66, 70
gravimeter, 66
Great Britain, 14, 30, 32
Great Valley, 12–13
Greece, *14,* 31, 64, *85*
ground-penetrating radar, 66
groundwater, 5, 10, 16, 24, 41, 49,

80, 82–83

grout, 70

Guilian, China, 28

Gulf of Mexico, 36, 46, 52, 53, 87

gypsum, 14, 43, 72

Hart's tongue fern, American, 54

Hawaii, 18

hay, 76

haystack hill, 28–29, *29*

Hidden River Cave, 80

hiker, 86–87, *87*

Homosassa River, 58–59

horse, 76

hydrologic, 40

hydrologist, 8, 66, 82

Ibex, 63

India, 62

Indiana, 17, 23, 32, 38, 41, 45, 51, 62, 64, 69, 73, 83

Indonesia, 76

Inverness, FL, 19

Ionian Islands, 14

iron ore, 38

Israel, 48

Italy, 52

Jamaica, 28, 44, 76

Japan, 6, 36, 76

Jeita Cave, 48

Jennings Cave, 86

Jerusalem, Israel, 48

joint, 14, 16, 42

Jordan, 62

Juniper Springs, 59

Kansas, 11

karren, 12

karst, 7, 11–16, 18, 20, 24, 26, 28–32, 34–35, 38, 40–48, 50–51, 59, 66–67, 69–70, 72, 74–75, 80, 82–83

Kauai, HI, 18

Kentucky, 5, 17, 31, 45, 70–71, 76, 80, 82, 85

kettle hole, 76

Key Largo, FL, 36

Kwangsi Province, China, 28

Lake Eaton, FL, 87

Lake Jackson, FL, *35*

lake, 5, 12, 22, 34, 35, 38–39, 40, 44, 46, 56, 58, 62, 86–87

Laos, 6

Lapis, 13

Lawrence of Arabia, 64

lead ore, 78

Lechuguilla Cave, 24

Lexington, KY, 5, 70

Li River, *28*

limestone pavement, 12

limestone, 14–16, 19, *23*, 26, 30, 33, 50, 54, 56, 83

Lincoln Caverns, 25

Little Salt Spring, 78

littoral, 18

livestock, 76, 80

Logan County, KY, 45

Loma Prieta, CA, 11

Long Beach, CA, 10

Los Angeles, CA, 10

losing stream, 32

Luray Caverns, *25*

Magnesium, 14

Maine, 6

Mallorca, 13

Mammoth Cave, 17, 25

manatee, *58*

manna grass, 57

Marg Pond, MO, 57

Marianna, FL, 33, 49

Martel, Edouard-Alfred, 80

Maryland, 31

mastodon, 86

Mayan, 64–65

Mediterranean, 6, 13

mesquite, 62

Mexico, 36, 46, 64, 65, 82

microclimate, 4

mine, 38, 42, 43, 78

mining, 38, 42, 43, 78

Miocene, 36

Missouri, 27, 32, 38, 78, 80

Mitchell Plateau, IN, 17, 51

mogote, 28

mollusk, 14

Montezuma's Well, AZ, 62

Moscow, 6

mosquito, 60

mountain, 28, 31, 85

Mud Hole Submarine Spring, 53

mullet, 58

NASA, 37, 39, 63–64

National Speleological Society, 85

natural bridge, 6, 29

Natural Bridge, VA, *28*

Nepal, 15

New Guinea, 28

New Jersey, 57

New Mexico, 6, 24, 46

New York, 52

nitrate, 80, 82

North America, 54

Nullabor Plain, Australia, 6, 64

Oak, 12

oasis, 48, *62, 63,* 64

Ocala National Forest, 59, 87

Ocala, FL, 75

Ohio, 64, 78

Okinawa, Japan, 36

Oligocene, 36

Oman, 62, 64

oolite, 14

Orange Lake, 44

Orlando, FL, 4, 21, 23, 68

oryx, 63

otter, 54

Ozarks, MO, 32

Pacific Ocean, 36

Paisley, FL, 57

Paleolithic, 64, 78

paleontologist, 8

Paxos, Greece, 14

peach, 60

Pecos River, 6

Pelopennese, Greece, 85

Pennsylvania, 12, 25, 78–79

pepino, 28

permafrost, 11

permeable, 14–15, 46, 50

pipeline, 11, 62, 72–73

pocket valley, 30

Pokhara, Nepal, 15

Poland, 29

polje, 31, 76, *77*

pollution as a result of
dumping, *80–84*
fertilizers, 76, 80, 84
fumes, 80
sewage, *81*

pollution, 74, 80, 82, 84–85

pond, 5, 11, 22, 31, *42*, 44, 56–58, 64

ponor, 31–32

ponore, 31–32

porous, 14–15, 87

potato, 76

pothole, 12

praying mantis, 57

pseudokarst, 18

Puerto Rico, 6, 7, 28, 82

Pushkar, India, 62

Raveling, 20, 84

re-breather, 47

recharge, 46

recreation, 9, 51, 86–87

Red Snapper Sink, 53

remediation, 70–71

resurgence, 30, 44

retention pond, *42, 75*

rice, 76

Riva Skocjan, Slovakia, 6

River Aire, 30

river, 6, 13, *15*, 15–16, 28, 30, *33*, 40–41, 44, 46, 48, 51, 59, 80, 82, 87

river, subterranean, 30, 48

Riversink, 32

Rosel, Kansas, 11

Roswell Aquifer, 46

Sahara Desert, 48

salamander, 54, 57, 60–60, *61*

saltwater intrusion, 37, 82–83

San Antonio, TX, 46

San Jose, CA, 10

sand, 8, 20, 22, 36, 38, 42, 66, 74, 78

Sanibel Island, FL, 53

Sarasota, FL, 78

Sargasso Sea, 59

Saudi Arabia, 63

Savannah, GA, 83

sea cave, 14, 18

seawater, 52, 58, 59, 82–83

sedimentary rock, 14

seismic detector, 66, 67

Seneca Caverns, 27

sewage, 80–81

sheep, 76

sheepshead, 58

Shelby County, AL, 21, 66, 72

Shenandoah Caverns, *26*

Shenandoah Valley, VA, 56, *57*

Silver Springs, 86

sink, 34–35, 55

sinkholes as a threat to
buildings, *5,* 8, *11, 20, 45, 68–69,*

74–75, *75*
   roads, *43*, 68, *72*
   pipelines, 68, 72–73, *73*
   vehicles, *38*
sinkholes, types of
   collapse, 18, 22, 64, 74, 76
   subsidence, 20, 22, 42
   solution-subsidence, 16, 22, 76
sinking stream, 30–33, *33*, *40*
sinking valley, 30
Sinking Valley, PA, 78–79
Sinks of Gandy, 31
Siwa Oasis, Egypt, *63*
skink, 9
Skyline Caverns, *27*
slate, 15
Slovenia, 6, 76, 77
Smoke Hole Caverns, *48*
snail, 58, 60
snapper, 53, 58
snook, 58
soil, 4, 12–14, 16, 20, 22, 36, 38, 40,
   42, 44, 66–67, 84, 85
solution pan, 31
solution pipe, 4, 16, 48
solution-subsidence, 16, 22, 76
sonar mapping, 47
Sonoran Desert, 62
South Africa, 43
space shuttle, 37, 39, 64
Spain, 7, 50
Spring Mill State Park, 45
spring vent, *40*
spring, 12, 30, 35, 40, 45–49, *50–53*,
   58, 59, 62–63, *63*, 82, *87*
Springs of Harub, 48
St. Louis, MO, 80

St. Marks River, *33*
stalactite, *27*
stalagmite, *27*
steephead, 30
stonewort, 56
stormwater, 74
stream, 13, 29–32, 41, 44, 46, 50–51,
   59
stream, underground, 84
submarine spring, 52–53
subsidence, 10–11, 16, 20, 67
sugar cane, 76
Suwannee River, 16
swallet, 31–32, 35, 82, 85
swallow hole, 31–32, 35, 82, 85
swimmer, 86–87
Sylacauga, AL, 5, 85
Taino, 78
Talahasochte, 56
Tallahassee, FL, 8, 43, 46
Tampa, FL, 42
Tampico, Mexico, 46
Tennessee, 54
Texas, 10, 19, 46
Thar Desert, 62
thermokarst, 11
tower karst, 28–29, *29*
toxic fumes, 80
travertine, *48*
troglobite, 60
troglophile, 54
trogloxene, 60
Truk Island, 36
U.S. Fish and Wildlife Service, 85
Ubar, 64
underwater radio, 47
underwater scooter, 47

Undiri, 64
United States, 21, 46
uvala, 30–31, *31*
Vietnam, 6
Vikos, Greece, 31
Virginia sneezeweed, 56
Virginia, 11, 25–27, 43, 45, 49, 56–57,
   72
Wakulla Springs, 47, 86
Waldron Camp, TX, 19
water cycle, 40, 41, 46
water scorpion, 62
water table, 4, 18, 23–24, 35, 40–44,
   46, 48, 56, 70, 80, 82–83
waterfall, 32, 55
Wekiwa Springs, 4, 23
well, 11, 42, 48, 62, 82–83
West Virginia, 27, 31–32, 48
wheat, 76
Whisper Rocks Cave, 25
Winter Park, FL, 20
Withlacoochee State Forest, 19
wolf, 54
Woodruff Dam, 40
Woodville Karst Plain Project, 47
Woodville Karst Plain, 46–47
worm, 54, 60
Yam, 76
Yangsuo, China, 28
Yorkshire, Great Britain, 30, 32
Yucatan Aquifer, 46
Yucatan Peninsula, Mexico, 46, 65, 82
Yugoslavia, 6, 30
Yunnan, China, 28
Zacatón, Mexico, 46
Zambia, 6
zinc, 78

Acknowledgments

I was first exposed to sinkholes and karst terrain after moving to Ocala, Florida, in the late 1970s and rediscovered my interest in the subject while researching mineral formations in central Pennsylvania. The advent of the Internet allowed me to ask questions of many experts in the field. I read through textbooks on karst at Pennsylvania State University and visited the Pennsylvania Geological Survey, where William Kochanov took the time to explain the mechanics of sinkhole formation and Richard Keen pulled library materials that furthered my education on the subject.

In 1996, several draft chapters intended for this book launched my career as a children's author. Focusing on broader topics of earth science, I laid this book aside while fulfilling my contract with Twenty First Century Books. I am thankful that June Cussen at Pineapple Press found my proposal appealing, bringing me back to this project.

In 2000, I put out a call to geologists around the country for photographs and information. Many responded and took the time to work with me: Joe McGregor, Trent Faust, and Pete Swarzenski, U.S. Geological Survey (USGS); Larry Dean, U.S. Fish and Wildlife Service; Harley Means, Florida Geological Survey; Sam Frushour, Indiana Geological Survey; David C. Kopaska-Merkel, Geological Survey of Alabama; Jim Currens, Kentucky Geological Survey; and David Hubbard, Virginia Department of Mines, Minerals and Energy, Division of Mineral Resources (VDMME/DMR).

Thanks to all of the photographers and researchers who responded to my e-mails and personal calls for contributions to this book. Dave Bunnell, editor of the *NSS News*, provided excellent foreign photos, as did David Hubbard from his own personal archives. James Rebmann provided an essential series of photos on sinkhole remediation. Mike Gentry at NASA's Lyndon B. Johnson Space Center helped tremendously by tracking down some hard-to-find space shuttle images. Historical photo recommendations came from James Cusick at the P. K. Yonge Library of Florida History, Department of Special Collections, George A. Smathers Libraries, University of Florida. The Florida State Archives provided images from their collection as well. And thanks to my mother, Linda Friend, who kept an archive of sinkhole-related newspaper clippings for me over the past five years.

As for review, thanks to fellow Florida Mineral Friends member Sam Upchurch, who suggested a few changes, and Rich Evans, who did my initial proofreading. Special thanks to my expert reader, Ernst H. Kastning, professor of geology at Radford University (Virginia) and a leading expert on karst and sinkholes. With his input, I feel confident in the quality of this book as an educational resource. Ernst clarified some of the key points, corrected my scientific errors, and provided additional resource material that I was able to incorporate into the book.

If you enjoyed reading this book, here are some other books from Pineapple Press on related topics. Ask your local bookseller for our books. For a complete catalog, write to Pineapple Press, P.O. Box 3889, Sarasota, FL 34230 or call 1-800-PINEAPL (746-3275). Or visit our website at www.pineapplepress.com.

African Americans in Florida by Maxine D. Jones and Kevin M. McCarthy. Profiles African Americans during four centuries of Florida history in brief essays. ISBN 1-56164-030-1 (hb); ISBN 1-56164-031-X (pb); ISBN 1-56164-045-X (teacher's manual)

Drawing Florida Wildlife by Frank Lohan. Whether you want to learn a new skill or improve your drawing skills, the easy directions in this guide will help you. Contains the clearest, easiest method yet for learning to draw birds, reptiles, amphibians, and mammals. Each section includes a partially finished drawing for you to complete. ISBN 1-56164-090-5 (pb)

Esmeralda and the Enchanted Pond by Susan Ryan. Delightful, full-color illustrations highlight the story of Esmeralda and her father, who visit a Florida forest during all four seasons and discover that there's a scientific explanation for everything that seems magical. An illustrated activity guide that conforms to the Sunshine State Standards is also available. ISBN 1-56164-236-3 (hb); ISBN 1-56164-247-9 (activity guide)

The Florida Water Story by Peggy Sias Lantz and Wendy A. Hale. Illustrates and describes many of the plants and animals that depend on the springs, rivers, beaches, marshes, and reefs in and around Florida, including corals, sharks, lobsters, alligators, manatees, birds, turtles, and fish. Suggests ways everyone can help protect Florida's priceless natural resources. ISBN 1-56164-099-9 (hb)

Florida's First People by Robin C. Brown. Filled with photos of replicas of technologies used by early peoples in their daily lives, this book brings to life the first humans who entered Florida about 12,000 years ago. Great for a budding archaeologist or historian! ISBN 1-56164-032-8 (hb)

Florida's Fossils by Robin Brown. Includes a complete identification section and insightful comments on the history of the fossil treasures you'll uncover. Budding archaeologists will appreciate updated maps and directions to some of the best fossil-hunting areas in Florida. ISBN 1-56164-114-6 (pb)

Giant Predators of the Ancient Seas by Judy Cutchins and Ginny Johnston. This book explores how scientists use fossil clues to learn about the lives and habitats of the most exciting sea animals that ever lived. Second in the Southern Fossil Discoveries series, this volume gives readers an in-depth, straightforward look at the giant creatures that prowled the waters of prehistory. Includes color photos and original paintings. ISBN 1-56164-237-1 (hb)

Ice Age Giants of the South by Judy Cutchins and Ginny Johnston. First in the Southern Fossil Discoveries series, this book chronicles up-to-date discoveries in the field of archaeology and describes how prehistoric animals looked, how they lived, and what they ate. Includes full-color photos of fossil bones, reconstructed skeletons, and lifelike models of extinct creatures. ISBN 1-56164-195-2 (hb)

Native Americans in Florida by Kevin M. McCarthy. Teaches about the many diverse Indian tribes in Florida from prehistoric times to the present. Also includes information about archaeology, an extensive glossary, and legends that teach moral lessons. ISBN 1-56164-181-2 (hb); ISBN 1-56164-182-0 (pb); ISBN 1-56164-188-X (teacher's manual)

The Young Naturalist's Guide to Florida by Peggy Sias Lantz and Wendy A. Hale. Complete with a glossary, this enticing book shows you where and how to look for Florida's most interesting natural features and creatures. Take it along on your next walk in the woods! ISBN 1-56164-051-4 (pb)